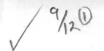

PS   Barksdale, Richard.
3515
.U274 Langston Hughes
Z615

DATE			

HIRAM KELLY BRANCH
6151 S. NORMAL BLVD.
CHICAGO, ILLINOIS 60621

Langston Hughes

THE POET AND HIS CRITICS

Langston Hughes

THE POET AND HIS CRITICS

RICHARD K. BARKSDALE

AMERICAN
LIBRARY
ASSOCIATION
CHICAGO
1977

THE POET AND HIS CRITICS

A series of volumes on the meaning of the critical writings on selected modern British and American poets.

Edited by CHARLES SANDERS, University of Illinois, Urbana

Robert Frost by Donald J. Greiner
William Carlos Williams by Paul L. Mariani
Dylan Thomas by R. B. Kershner, Jr.

The following are reprinted by permission of Harold Ober Associates, Incorporated: "Bad Man," © 1927 by Alfred A. Knopf, Inc., renewed; "Ballad of the Landlord," © 1951 by Langston Hughes; "The Cat and the Saxophone," © 1926 by Alfred A. Knopf, renewed; "Christ in Alabama," © 1932 by Langston Hughes, renewed; "Dimout in Harlem," © 1947 by Langston Hughes, renewed; "Dream Boogie," © 1951 by Langston Hughes; "Dreams," © 1932 by Alfred A. Knopf, Inc., renewed; "Good Morning, Revolution," © 1932 by Langston Hughes, renewed; "Goodby Christ," © 1932 by Langston Hughes, renewed; "Hard Luck," © 1927 by Alfred A. Knopf, Inc., renewed; "Jester," © 1926 by Alfred A. Knopf, Inc., renewed; "Juice Joint: Northern City," © 1949 by Langston Hughes, renewed; "Lady's Boogie," © 1951 by Langston Hughes; "Let America Be America Again," © 1938 by Langston Hughes, renewed; "Likewise," © 1951 by Langston Hughes; "Live and Let Live," © 1951 by Langston Hughes; "Madam and the Charity Child," © 1959 by Langston Hughes; "A New Song," © 1938 by Langston Hughes, renewed; "Oppression," © 1947 by Langston Hughes, renewed; "Park Bench," © 1938 by Langston Hughes, renewed; "Pride," © 1938 by Langston Hughes, renewed; "Revolution," © 1934 by Langston Hughes, renewed; "The Same," © 1932 by Langston Hughes, renewed; "Scottsboro," © 1932 by Langston Hughes, renewed; "Sliver," © 1951 by Langston Hughes, renewed; "Southern Negro Speaks," © 1941 by Langston Hughes, renewed; "Today," © 1947 by Alfred A. Knopf, Inc., renewed; "Wine-o," © 1951 by Langston Hughes.
Grateful acknowledgment is made to Alfred A. Knopf, Inc., for use of the selections from the copyrighted works of Langston Hughes.

LIBRARY OF CONGRESS CATALOGING IN PUBLICATION DATA
Barksdale, Richard.
    Langston Hughes, the poet and his critics.
    (The Poet and his critics)
    Bibliography: p.
    1. Hughes, Langston, 1902–1967—Poetic works.
2. Hughes, Langston, 1902–1967—Criticism and interpretation—History.   I. Title.
PS3515.U274Z615   811'.5'2   77-8599
ISBN 0-8389-0237-5

Copyright © 1977 by the American Library Association

Printed in the United States of America

To my grandchildren, Nikki
and Jay;
To my youngest, Calvin Philip;
and
To my wife, Mildred—
  with reverence for the past,
  love for the present, and
  hope for the future.

Contents

Preface

The purpose of this study is to assess what the critics have written in response to the poetry of Langston Hughes over the forty-seven-year period of his literary career. Necessarily, there are limitations on the scope of such a study—some mandated by the nature of the materials and some self-imposed by the author. First, the study focuses on Hughes's poetry, which represents only a small portion of the productive range of this prolific and versatile writer. According to Donald Dickinson's *A Bio-Bibliography of Langston Hughes, 1902-1967* (1967), Hughes published forty-eight volumes, but only fifteen, or slightly less than one-third, were volumes of poetry. This suggests that in terms of sheer man-hours, he devoted more time to writing fiction and drama and to editing anthologies than he did to writing poetry. Thus the argument is often advanced that a discussion of Langston Hughes the poet presents Langston Hughes the writer only from a very narrow perspective. On the other hand, Hughes began as a poet, starting as an elementary class poet in his school in Lincoln, Illinois, and senior class poet in Cleveland, Ohio, and then, at age nineteen, publishing "The Negro Speaks of Rivers" in the *Crisis* in 1921. Moreover, the 1920s were almost exclusively devoted to poetry; he won a prize for "Weary Blues" in 1925, and then published two books of poetry before the decade closed. And in every decade thereafter he published one or two volumes of poetry as well as a plethora of occasional poems in a large number of periodicals. In the end his career closed as it had begun with the publication of *The Panther and the Lash,* his final volume of poetry. So poetry was never a neglected mistress, despite the time devoted to other kinds of literary ventures and interests.

Nevertheless, the question is often raised whether a writer of formidable output like Hughes can be justly assessed by looking at only one aspect of his work. For instance, he treated the mulatto theme in a poem, in a short story, in a play, and in an opera. Can one study his treatment of this theme in one genre only and ignore the other three genres? Or can one discuss Hughes's essentially comic approach to black urban blues in poetical terms only, and ignore that marvelous comic creation Jess B. Semple? The only argument for a single-genre approach to Hughes is that poetry is a distinctive self-identifying genre. As critics as early as Aristotle and Horace have said, certain literary qualities and approaches are poetic and others are not. Conversely, not even in a narrative poem can one give all of the narrative detail found in the setting, plot, and characterization of a short story. Thus, although Madam Alberta K. Johnson is just as much a product of Hughes's comic genius as Jess B. Semple, Madam Johnson, presented in small fragmented vignettes, is a much less fully-formed character than Simple, who is fleshed out in copious narrative detail. His character, moving from incident to incident, develops, grows, and assumes a personality that reflects a predictable pattern of continuity. So, in practical and technical terms, Hughes as poet is different from Hughes as novelist or dramatist or essayist. Admittedly, his subject matter is always the same—the struggle of America's black citizen to achieve full citizenship—but his method and manner necessarily changed as he moved from genre to genre.

For this reason, the decision was made to limit this study to an assessment of the critics of Hughes's poetry, although there is a large amount of very challenging critical writing in several languages on the Simple stories. It is hoped that in some yet-to-be-published definitive assessment of Hughes as man and writer, this large amount of critical writing on the Simple stories can be evaluated and placed in proper literary perspective. Certainly, Hughes's achievement in developing the character of Jess B. Semple is of singular import in the annals of Afro-American literary history.

Some comment should be made here on the method and approaches used in this study. First, because Hughes as poet was so completely engrossed in the particular and the contemporary, every effort is made to define chronological settings and to give the mood and temper of the various periods of his active literary career. To some readers, particularly those of the New Critic persuasion to whom historical background is anathema, the devotion of time and space to definitions of trends and descriptions of backgrounds would seem to be either inordinately detailed or absolutely unnecessary. But different times induced different reactions and responses in both poet and critic. Hughes's subject matter in the politically leftist 1930s and the critical reaction to his leftist poetry were different from what occurred in the 1950s or 1960s. So every effort has been made to fit the poet within a contextual time frame.

Secondly, an effort has also been made to provide useful critical introductions to Hughes's poetry in each chapter before presenting the reactions of the critics to his poetry. Inevitably, there are broad and often gaping differences between what the critics have written and the critical introductions provided by the author. Undeniably, the mixture of approaches and interpretations is good; the fact that the poetry of Langston Hughes is provocative of critical dialogue is good in and of itself. For Hughes, as the leading Afro-American poet of this century, has not always commanded the kind of critical attention which his work has merited.

After the presentation of statements and judgments of the critics, an effort is then made to assess these statements and judgments, and, insofar as possible, compare and contrast critical approaches. The net result of this critical method is to see Langston Hughes as poet with greater clarity.

Another feature of this study is that it does not claim to be definitive and all-encompassing. Many reviewers and/or critics receive no mention simply because, in the opinion of the author, their reviews or critical observations add little or nothing to Hughesian critical lore. In this connection, it should be pointed out that Dickinson's *Bio-Bibliography* is used as a very reliable bibliographical source but not as a critical work, since the principal objective of this text is bibliographical and not critical. Also, not all of Hughes's poetry is discussed; only those poems that incited some measure of critical response are treated.

One beneficial by-product of this study is the light thrown on the contributions of certain critics. Alain Locke, for instance, attended to Hughes's development as a poet from the beginning up to the early 1950s, and his comments on the poet say much about his own philosophy of creative literature. Similarly, the critical statements of Jean Wagner, the French critic and author of *Les Poètes Nègres Des États-Unis*, assume an almost focal significance in some phases of this study. It is in a sense ironical that the most sustained critical analysis of America's foremost black poet should be provided by a non-American caucasian. The irony is intensified when one realizes the extent to which Hughes's poetry was so inextricably involved with social and moral issues that were peculiarly American. As will be seen, Wagner attempts to erect bridges of understanding between his French background and Hughes's black urban American background. As I suggest, he appears to understand the later Hughes better than the earlier.

I should also like to note in this context the importance of black literary journals like *Opportunity*, *Crisis*, *Phylon*, and the *CLA Journal* in providing channels for the flow of Afro-American literary criticism. Of particular importance are the annual literary surveys in *Opportunity* in the 1930s and 1940s, and in *Phylon* in the later decades. Of course, annual literary surveys are not usually a source for perceptive or perspicacious literary comment, but those written by Alain Locke more than often fill the critical bill.

Finally, in this chronological assessment of Hughes's poetry, although there is a discernible dialogue between certain critics and the author, there is no perceptible dialogue between the poet and these critics. This is probably the way it should be. Hughes's biographical record indicates that, regardless of his forthright response to his critics in "The Negro Writer and the Racial Mountain" in the 1920s, he was not in continuous contention with his critics, however adverse and disapproving they were on occasion. Apparently his was the kind of congenial temperament that assured him some measure of immunity from many of the needling adversities that so easily beset authors in our culture. This is not to say that Hughes was less trouble-ridden than other mortals; in *The Big Sea* and *I Wonder as I Wander* and "My Adventures as a Social Poet" in *Phylon*, he recounts many troubling episodes resulting from racial discrimination and prejudice. But, unless his yet unpublished letters are filled with rancorous responses to disapproving critics, one must believe that Hughes wrote his poetry with his eye on a particular event, issue, or person and was either oblivious of, or indifferent to, adverse criticism.

I wish to express my thanks and gratitude to the following: Professor Charles Sanders, a colleague and friend who, as editor of this series, has been persistently helpful and encouraging; to the Research Board of the University of Illinois at Urbana-Champaign from whom I received two grants that helped me initiate this project; to the director and staff of the Center of Advanced Study at UIUC who provided opportunity and space and the proper scholarly environment to get the work done; to Irene Wahlfeldt and Anita Brown who assisted in preparing the manuscript; and last but not least, to Mildred, my wife, without whose patience, understanding, and support this study could never have been brought to completion.

CHAPTER 1

A Writer for All Seasons

As the foremost black American author of the twentieth century, Langston Hughes has received his full share of accolades and biographical tributes since his death in 1967. These he fully merited because of his forty-seven years of unwavering dedication to the responsibilities of authorship and his calm acceptance of the joys, sorrows, self-doubts, and occasional self-flagellation accompanying that kind of dedication. In many respects, the role of a self-declared black man of letters is predictably hazardous, even in the enlightened America of recent times. During his long years of authorship, Hughes had to serve as the literary spokesman for a divided and insecure racial minority—a minority made more paranoid by every passing day's record of covert discrimination or overt racial violence. At the same time, he had to walk the razor's edge of general acceptability by America's racial majority, protesting the country's racism yet endorsing its democratic promise. Such acceptability was a prerequisite for getting his work published, and failure to have done this would have turned his years of rich productivity into years of silent neglect.

Fortunately, Hughes survived all of these tensions of authorship, and he is now fondly remembered as a remarkably urbane, self-possessed, and relatively unruffled man of letters. He was, in the face of all that befell him, consistently affable and incredibly unflappable. Indeed, on one occasion in 1951, amid considerable heated interracial and intraracial controversy, the poet wrote of himself:

> I play it cool
> And dig all jive
> That's the reason
> I stay alive.

The critical implications of this brief and somewhat slangy poem will be discussed further in this study. Suffice it to say now that at least one critic views the poem as an important credal statement defining the poet's cool detachment from many of the events which swirled about him during the last two decades of his life.

Hughes's poetical career began when he was a young teenager in Lincoln, Illinois. In the grammar school of that small, semirural, middle Illinois town, he was elected class poet at the tender age of thirteen. After moving to Cleveland, he continued to write poetry imitative in style and content of that of Carl Sandburg. These few lines by a teenage Hughes describing the grinding misery of the steel mill laborer clearly reveal a Sandburgian influence:

> The mills
> That grind and grind
> That grind out steel
> And grind away the lives
> Of men . . .
>
> The mills
> Grinding new steel
> Old men.

After graduation as senior class poet from Cleveland's Central High School, Hughes blossomed into publication when several of his poems were published in the *Brownie Book*, a junior magazine of the National Association for the Advancement of Colored People (NAACP) that appeared monthly from January, 1920 to December, 1921. Following these initial efforts Hughes then published "The Negro Speaks of Rivers" in the June, 1921, issue of *Crisis*, the official journal of the NAACP. For a young man of nineteen, this was a singular literary achievement.

The *Crisis*, under the literary editorship of Jessie Fauset, future novelist and poet in her own right, quickly exploited the burgeoning talents of the young writer. Following the appearance of "The Negro Speaks of Rivers," the *Crisis* published many of the poems that were to appear in Hughes's first book of poems, *The Weary Blues* (1926). One of the more famous of these early poems was "Mother to Son," a dramatic monologue proving the young poet's early competence in this particular poetical genre:

> Well, son, I'll tell you:
> Life for me ain't been no crystal stair.
> It's had tacks in it,
> And splinters,

And boards torn up,
And places with no carpet on the floor . . .
But all the time
I'se been a-climbin' on,
And reachin landin's,
And turning corners, . . .
So boy, don't you turn back.
Don't you set down on the steps
'Cause you finds it's kinder hard.

This poem and others of this same category indicate that Hughes very early in his career had developed the ability to project himself imaginatively into many dramatic roles. On occasion, the emerging persona, like the enduring matriarch of "Mother to Son," is presented with all the dramatic skill and power of a seasoned and experienced poet.

Unfortunately, Hughes's rising career as a young poet was interrupted by an academically disastrous freshman year at Columbia University in 1921-22 and by the frustrating consequences of that experience. In the agonizing aftermath to this year, Hughes drifted from one odd job to another in the New York City area; and then, in 1923, he signed on board a merchant ship as a kitchen helper or mess steward and, for almost two years, traveled to Africa and Europe. However, the interruption to his poetic career was temporary; for when he returned in late 1924 and took up residence with his mother in Washington, D.C., he resumed his writing and received considerable publicity as the "Negro busboy poet" of the Wardman Park Hotel. This title was given him by Vachel Lindsay who had had opportunity to read some of Hughes's poetry. But the man who actually prepared the way for Hughes's first book of poetry was Carl Van Vechten. The latter read "The Weary Blues" after it won an *Opportunity* magazine prize in 1925 as the best poem written by a Negro in that year. Impressed, Van Vechten then read all of Hughes's poems and recommended them for immediate publication to Blanche and Alfred Knopf, his close friends and owners of one of New York's fast-rising publishing firms. The result was *The Weary Blues*.

Not all of the poems in this initial volume by Hughes are blues poems, although the volume's title might so indicate. The poems in this collection represent the kind of thematic mixture which was to characterize most of Hughes's subsequent published work in poetry. There are poems like "Caribbean Sunset" and "Young Sailor" reflecting the poet's seaborne odyssey in 1923 and 1924. There are powerful dramatic monologues like "Mother to Son" and "Young Prostitute." There are poems about racial conflict like "Cross" and "Lament for Dark Peoples." And there are poems which explore the dream motif and its effects on the black experience—poems like "Dream Variations" and "The Dream-Keeper." It should be noted here that Hughes never abandoned emphasis on the importance of the dream and that his concern led him eventually to his 1951 work, *Montage of a Dream Deferred*.

Unfortunately, the poet's next volume, *Fine Clothes to the Jew* (1927), contains no such mixture of poetic themes but concentrates almost solely on folk urban blues. There are one or two racial conflict poems like "Mulatto" and "Brass Spittoons," but the poet's objective appears to be to recapture all of the bluesy exuberance of black life in the big city. There are poems about crap games, storefront churches, cabarets, prize fighters, jazz bands, prostitutes, and gypsies. As noted in greater detail below, the general tone of Hughes's poems in this volume affronted and alienated an important segment of the black upper middle classes. Much of the adverse criticism came from that stratum of the black intelligentsia known informally as the "talented tenth." This phrase, descriptive of a leadership potential in black America, was originally used by W. E. B. Du Bois in his *Souls of Black Folk* in 1903. Unfortunately, by the 1920s the term "talented tenth" had become synonymous with the smugly respectable brown and beige upper middle-class society whose members had arrogated unto themselves the responsibility of leading the rest of black America into an acceptable form of racial integration. This group had also lost all effective contact with the black lower classes and tended to view their activities and interests as major impediments to full integration. Accordingly, members of the "talented tenth" disapproved of any black cultural expressions in art and literature which were not acceptable to the most respectable echelons of white society. Their insistence on an impeccable morality in theme and statement in turn infuriated young black writers like Hughes, McKay, and Toomer; for these writers were caught in the exciting web of the new naturalism that emphasized the sensual, the primitive, the carnal, and the sordid. As mentioned below, Hughes expressed his opposition to the "talented tenth" approach to literature in his essay "The Negro Artist and the Racial Mountain," published in the *Nation* in 1926.

Following the publication in 1930 of *Not Without Laughter*, Hughes's first novel, the young writer produced four slim volumes of poetry during the next two years: *Dear Lovely Death* (1931), *The Negro Mother* (1931), *The Dream-Keeper and Other Poems*

(1932), and *Scottsboro Limited* (1932). Of these four, *The Dream-Keeper* is the largest and contains several poems published earlier: "The Negro Speaks of Rivers," "Mexican Market Woman," and "Mother to Son." *Scottsboro Limited* stands out in this group as Hughes's first piece of writing that aligned him politically with international Communism. The balance of the decade of the thirties was devoted to fiction and drama until *A New Song* appeared in 1938. The poems in this last short volume of thirty-one pages clearly reflect a strong Communist influence, and the fact that the publisher was the International Workers Order is further proof of a less-than-casual relationship between Hughes and international Communism.

In *Shakespeare in Harlem* (1942) Hughes returned to the poetic mixture of urban blues and racial protest found in *The Weary Blues* sixteen years before. But in 1942 the emphasis was more on lamentation rather than on celebration. Bitterness drenches the lines of "Lover's Return" and "Early Evening Quarrel"; and there is no doubt that black Harlem is still in the grip of an economic depression in 1942. All is not unalloyed pessimism, however; poems like "Sylvester's Dying Bed" and "Morning After" give some evidence that Hughes's comic vision is growing and that he is beginning to be aware that black urban blues is a comedy etched in misery and a misery etched in comedy.

Freedom's Plow and *Jim Crow's Last Stand* (1943) were both wartime poetic utterances, noting the conflict between America's racial promises and practices. After the war ended and America moved into the cold war of the late 1940s, Hughes produced two more volumes of poetry—*Fields of Wonder* (1947) and *One-Way Ticket* (1949). The poems in the 1947 volume say little about black Harlem. Instead, there are nostalgic lines about good living and high thinking during the poet's stay at Carmel, California, in 1932 right after he returned from Russia. On the other hand, *One-Way Ticket* offers the same blend of urban blues and racial protest poetry found in the earlier *Shakespeare in Harlem*, with one significant exception. The volume begins with a section entitled "Madam to You." Here Hughes presents Madam Alberta K. Johnson, a prototype of the enterprising black woman who lives, laughs, and loves in the heart of the black ghetto and survives with a good-humored dignity. Two generations removed from the black matriarch of slavery times who survived an earlier chaos and confusion, Madam Johnson has the same resourcefulness and determination. Her character and that of other folk vignettes in this volume show the growth and enrichment of Hughes's comic vision at this time.

The poet's next volume of poems, *Montage of a Dream Deferred*, is actually one long poem in six sections devoted exclusively to black Harlem—its frustrations, its anger, its joys, and its sorrows. The pathos of poverty and the small desperate amenities of life in the ghetto are the subjects of *Montage*. The result is an in-depth picture of an American urban ghetto at the beginning of the fifth decade of the twentieth century. Hopes and aspirations have vanished; dreams are "deferred" and unfulfilled. Black laughter in the main has given away to black anger. Similarly, the poet's mood and matter have darkened since *Shakespeare in Harlem* or *One-Way Ticket*. An interesting feature of *Montage* is Hughes's attempt to insinuate into the structure and theme of these poems the mode and manner of bebop jazz which became so popular in post-World War II New York City.

After 1951, Hughes's career as a writer underwent considerable change. First, he was sufficiently encouraged by the remarkable success of the captivating Simple stories to spend a large amount of time on continuing them and on developing his short prose fiction. Next he undertook to tell the black man's history and culture in all of its variety and color. But as his years drew to a close, there was still time for poetry. He published *Selected Poems* in 1959, *Ask Your Mama* in 1961, and *The Panther and the Lash* in 1967. The poems in *Ask Your Mama* continue in the vein of those in *Montage* and attempt to link the media of music and poetry. As a consequence, many of the poems in this volume are avant-garde in tone and meaning and remarkably au courant for a man of Hughes's age. By 1961, the poet was fifty-nine years old and had been writing for forty years.

The Panther and the Lash brought Hughes's writing career full circle; in a sense, he ended almost as he had begun—publishing a mélange of poems of protest, poems on Africa, folk vignettes, and poems celebrating the black life-style. But the category of poems that had been a Hughesian trademark—the poem blending racial humor and protest—was missing from this last volume. Indeed, the 1960s were not years of jubilation and joy; and Hughes, blending with these times, sought to reflect the tension and turmoil of the period in his final volume.

Thus, the thematic content of Hughes's several volumes of poetry published over a period of almost fifty years changed little, with the exception of the poems of political protest and leftist content in the 1930s. Also, the poet's continuing emphasis on innovative forms and structures changed little throughout the years; he strove through various means to make his free verse break through barriers of poetic tradition. It will be seen that Hughes's nontraditional poetic structure never provoked the kind of outcry that his nontraditional content did.

More is needed to preface a study of the critical reaction to the poetry of Hughes than a brief overview of his poetical writings. Indeed, three matters have significant background relevance in any assessment of this black writer. These are his penchant for extensive travel wherever and whenever ports beckoned or adventure summoned; his high literary productivity in many genres; and his spiritual and psychic involvement with Harlem. Which of the three is the most important is difficult to determine, for in a sense all three complement each other. Undoubtedly, Hughes became a better writer because of the breadth of his travel; for, assuredly, knowledge of man's woe in Tashkent or in Shanghai helps one to understand man's woe in Harlem or in Watts. And, because of the extended range of his experiences in many different lands, the Harlem poet found more subjects to write about and more ways to assess the problem-seared existence of homo sapiens. Finally, Harlem remained the central setting for all of his writing because this section of Manhattan was the American black man's literary, cultural, and social mecca—the spot where a poet whose primary concern was the solution of America's race problem would have to implant the fixed leg of the compass of his experience. Like Tennyson's Ulysses, Langston Hughes became a part of all that he experienced; but he always carried with him the jazz and blues records and record player which helped him to stay tuned into Harlem, his home.

The story of some of his travels is told in his two autobiographies, *The Big Sea* (1940) and *I Wonder as I Wander* (1956). Both have a limited span, *The Big Sea* relating his travels and experiences up to his twenty-ninth year, and *I Wonder as I Wander* recounting his travels thereafter up to his thirty-fifth year. Thus, the years of travel that Hughes described in his two autobiographies run roughly from 1921 to 1937. This is not to imply that he did not continue to travel after 1937 and that these post-1937 experiences did not have a substantial effect on his writing. After 1937 there were trips to Spain and other places on the European continent; there were trips to China; and there were annual lecture and poetry-reading tours throughout the United States. After 1950, the early involvement with Caribbean and African cultures broadened and deepened and this development had an abiding effect on his subject matter and general political and racial orientation.

The critical reception accorded his first autobiographical accounting was generally favorable, despite Blanche Knopf's initial disclaimer that the manuscript was "too full of Carl [Van Vechten],

Thurman, Toomer, Hurston, etc." Richard Wright, reviewing *The Big Sea* in the *New Republic* (Oct. 28, 1940), praised the work. In particular he liked Hughes's self-portrait as a far-ranging "cultural ambassador" for black Americans. As a fellow black author, Wright praised Hughes for "creating a realistic literature of the Negro" and mastering "a range of artistic interest and expression possessed by no other writer of his time." Ralph Ellison's review in the *New Masses* (Oct. 1940) was somewhat more restrained; he liked the picaresque novel effect of *The Big Sea* but thought its author had not included enough analysis and comment to explain how a sensitive black American like Hughes could attain "a heightened consciousness of a world" filled with racial hostility and adversity. Similarly, Alain Locke, in his annual review of Negro literature in *Opportunity* (Jan. 1941), thought that the poet's narrative of his early life and travels had an "irresponsible charm"; but, in Locke's opinion, there was too much "adventure" and not enough analysis of the significance of that adventure. He also thought that too many of *The Big Sea*'s anecdotes were "glossed over" and at times only "superficially entertaining." It is interesting to note that no reviewer came forward to quibble about so young a man writing his travel memoirs without the seasoning that comes from middle-aged meditation or from the wisdom of senescence. After all, had not Frederick Douglass written his *Narrative of His Life* in 1845 at the age of twenty-eight, giving an account of his years of trauma and adventure and daring as a slave? Therefore, could not a young black writer a century later write about his years of trauma and adventure and daring as a free man, bedeviled though he was by the network of Jim-Crowism that he encountered in his travels?

Just as Douglass had followed up his *Narrative* with a fuller version of his experiences in *My Bondage and My Freedom* in 1855, Hughes provided a further accounting in *I Wonder as I Wander*. This second volume of his autobiography was treated much less kindly by reviewers and by his critical reading public. In the first place, when Blanche Knopf saw the manuscript in 1949, she refused to sanction its publication and explained her reasons in a very kind letter to Hughes. She felt that it was too much of a miscellaneous travelogue, with too little of the author in it and far too many "other people" congregating in strange places. This thought was in a sense echoed in a *Herald Tribune* review by Saunders Redding who asserted that *I Wonder as I Wander* was not only a travelogue but in it "neither events or people are seen in depth." Actually, as one views the matter in retrospect, the timing of the publication of *I Wonder as I Wander* could not have been worse. Although the social and political phenomenon known as McCarthyism had in a sense disappeared by 1956, men and their ideas were still shadowed by its insidious afterglow. More importantly, the cold war was still a frigid certainty in 1956, and a book relating incidents favorable to the Russians or Communism was not welcome ideological fare for the American reading public. Not only did Hughes's autobiography describe in detail his 1932 trip to Russia, but at points in his description of his sojourn in Tashkent and in Uzbekistan, deep in the Asiatic reaches of the Soviet Union, the black poet seemed to be implying that it was far better to be a brown Uzbek than a black American. One can also surmise that his graphic account of his involvement in the Spanish Civil War and his obvious sympathy for the Loyalist and Communist forces were not as palatable to a wary American public in 1956 as they might have been in the early 1940s. The *Baltimore Afro-American*, a black newspaper, had in 1938 asked Hughes to serve as a reporter and observer of the bloody conflict; but, amid the bombs and shellfire, the poet found it difficult to remain neutral and objective in his reaction to Spain's civil turmoil. Moreover, his friend and fellow poet Federico García Lorca, the Spanish poet whose *Gypsy Ballads* he was to translate in 1951, had been killed by Fascist forces early in the war. So *I Wonder as I Wander* revealed a Langston Hughes who was partial and sympathetic toward the Soviet Union and fully supportive of the Communist cause in the Spanish Civil War. It should be pointed out here that Langston Hughes never joined the Communist party for two reasons, one serious and one facetious. The serious reason was his belief that artists and authors were not permitted freedom of expression in a Communist society. The facetious reason was that jazz was condemned as "decadent capitalistic music" in a Communist society and hence outlawed, and the poet thought that he could not survive without jazz.

To the discerning eye *I Wonder as I Wander* revealed something else which may have accounted for the book's relatively poor reception by the American reading public, particularly by the conservative segment (the book sold less than three thousand copies in the first two years). As Hughes recounted some of the details of his poetry-reading tours throughout the South (started, incidentally, at the behest of Mary McLeod Bethune), he at times became the angry racial militant, often distilling his anger into poetic statements full of chilling irony and sarcasm. The plight of the innocent Scottsboro boys, almost lynched in 1931 and then jailed for many years without "due process," particularly infuriated him. After visiting them at Kilby Prison while on a poetry-reading stop at

Tuskegee Institute, he very angrily dipped his pen and wrote a poem entitled "Christ in Alabama," which became one of the four poems of *Scottsboro Limited*.

Christ is a nigger,
Beaten and Black
Oh, bare your back!

Mary is His mother:
Mammy of the South,
Silence your mouth.

God is His father:
White master above,
Grant him your love.

Most holy bastard
Of the bleeding mouth,
    Nigger Christ
    On the cross
    Of the South.

When, at the invitation of Paul Green and Guy Johnson, Hughes promised to read his poetry at the University of North Carolina and this poem was published in the campus newspaper to advertise his coming, Chapel Hill quickly changed from a quiet academic retreat to a town boiling with potential riot. Despite threats of violence, the tour-reading poet fulfilled his obligation, but that ended poetry-reading engagements at white southern universities.

Notwithstanding crises of this kind, Langston Hughes continued to be a traveling man. In his bibliographical essay on Hughes (*CLA Journal*, June 1968), Therman O'Daniel stated that by 1951 Hughes had made seven cross-country poetry-reading tours. Inevitably, the extent of his traveling broadened his range of interests and enabled him to meet many writers from all over the world. During his rather lengthy sojourn in Russia, for instance, he met and had a fruitful professional association with Arthur Koestler, who at that time was a German Communist and very critical of Russian inefficiency. Similarly, his travels to the Caribbean resulted in endearing friendships with Nicolás Guillén, the Cuban mulatto poet; with Jacques Roumain, the famous Haitian author of *Gouverneurs de la Rosée*; and with Réne Piquion, a Haitian scholar who not only assisted Hughes in translating Roumain's famous novel but who wrote a biography of Hughes in 1940. From these experiences also came his play *Troubled Island*, which was produced by the Gilpin Players in Cleveland in 1935-36. His travels to Africa introduced him to the Senegalese poets Léopold Senghor and David Diop and eventually brought him to a place of honor at the Negro World Arts Festival at Dakar in the spring of 1966.

He also, through his travels, expanded his reach as a writer. During the long Moscow winter of 1932, for instance, he discovered the short stories of D. H. Lawrence and, using them as a general model, eventually produced his own *The Ways of White Folks* (1934). His Caribbean and African literary friendships proved to be invaluable in his work as a translator of works in Spanish and French which reflected some aspect of the black experience in other lands. With the assistance of Piquion and in collaboration with Professor Mercer Cook, Hughes produced *The Masters of the Dew* (1947), a translation of Roumain's greatest work. Ben Carruthers collaborated with him in translating Nicolás Guillén's *Cuba Libre* (1948). With assistance from many of García Lorca's friends during shell-filled days and bombed-out nights in Madrid, Hughes translated Lorca's *Gypsy Ballads* (1951). The poet also translated selected poems by Léon Damas, a native of Guyana and, along with Léopold Senghor and Aimé Césaire, one of the early formulators of the creed of *Négritude*. As mentioned earlier, Hughes was also friendly with David Diop and translated some of his poems for publication in his edition of *Poems from Black Africa* (1963). One of Hughes's most interesting literary friendships was with the Latin American poet Gabriela Mistral, who, in 1945, had the unique distinction of being the first Latin American writer to receive the Nobel Prize in literature. The Harlem poet translated her poems and then published them in *Selected Poems of Gabriela Mistral* (1957). John F. Matheus's "Langston Hughes as Translator" (*CLA Journal*, June 1968) provides an excellent summary of this aspect of the poet's career.

Thus, Langston Hughes's friendships with literary persons of other backgrounds and cultures challenged him to new endeavors as a literary practitioner and enriched his literary perspective. Throughout his years of travel, however, his primary literary concern continued to be the explication of the black experience in America. He strove in many ways to elucidate this concern—through his writing, extensive lecturing, participation on discussion panels, and television and radio interviews. Inevitably, he achieved his maximum effect through his writing, and there was no genre that he did not employ in his attempt to attain his objective. Therman O'Daniel (1968) states that Hughes's "mastery of a multiplicity of forms made him one of the most versatile American authors of the 20th century."

Indeed, his volume and variety of output are incredible by any standard. From his high school days until his death in 1967 poetry was admittedly his favorite and principal genre of literary expression—poetry reflecting many styles, techniques, and novel interpretive approaches to the American black experience. However, as his career developed, he began to employ other genres to suggest racial solutions, protest racial conditions, and illuminate some of the ironic implications of continued racial confrontation in America. He wrote fiction, including novels, short stories, children's stories, and five volumes of the Simple stories. He wrote drama, including full-length plays, one-act plays, opera librettos, gospel song-plays, and one screenplay. He wrote histories, including pictorial histories of black American heroes and entertainers, histories of jazz for young people, histories of the black man in the West Indies and in Africa. He wrote biographies: *Famous American Negroes* (1954) and *Famous Negro Music-Makers* (1955). He edited anthologies of the literary output of black writers in America, Africa, and the Caribbean Islands. He compiled *The Book of Negro Humor* (1966) and, with the assistance of Arna Bontemps, *The Book of Negro Folklore* (1959). He wrote radio and television scripts and lyrics for dramatic musicals. He wrote critical articles for periodicals—for the *Saturday Review of Literature*, *Phylon*, the *New Republic*, *Freedomways*. He made recordings for Columbia Records, Folkway Records, and Caedmon Records.

In the meantime, as Hughes poured out his many volumes, others wrote about him. They wrote short essays on his poetry, long essays on his drama, doctoral dissertations on his fiction, and incisively critical essays on the Simple stories. These essays in criticism were written in America, France, Denmark, Germany, the Soviet Union, and the islands of the Caribbean. Sometimes, the essays were not critical analyses of his literary work but somewhat effusive personal tributes to a man who had proven himself to be "a writer for all seasons." At other times the essays were angry attacks, charging Hughes with high crimes and misdemeanors against the American way or the Christian church or the black and white and brown middle classes. Such an essay was Elizabeth Staples's "Langston Hughes: Malevolent Force," published in *American Mercury* in 1959. Ms. Staples charged Hughes with being a dispenser of "depravity and obscenity"; a "sly and witty" master of innuendo and double entendres; an advocate of miscegenation; an avid pro-Communist and loyal friend of Communist enemies of the American way; and a subtle humorist who used the voice of Simple to foist his evil and corrupting thoughts on the American public. As will be seen in other chapters of this study devoted to analysis of the critical reactions to his poetry, by 1959 Langston Hughes had long become accustomed to being considered "a malevolent force."

Despite his life of movement, travel, and involvement in many activities in several countries, the story of Langston Hughes as writer began, ended, and played out its principal scenes in Harlem. In a sense this was to be expected, for all black writers flocked to Harlem during the 1920s. There they found a racial esprit and an air of promise absent from all of America's other urban areas where blacks fleeing the South tended to congregate. For the Harlem of the 1920s had broad and spacious avenues untouched by the racial rioting that had scarred the old Tenderloin District during Dunbar's day. Nor had Harlem known the bloodletting of the riots of Chicago or East St. Louis. For newcomers from the South, East, and West, Harlem was a place of bright refuge and a haven from the despair, fear, and oppression that hovered over the "spooktowns" of other northern cities.

Harlem as fact and symbol influenced the poetry of Hughes in many ways. In *The Weary Blues* the poem "Jazzonia" tells the reader that Harlem is in reality "Jazz town"—a place of the frantic drum beat; whirling, hip-shaking dancers; and bluesy, hazy cabarets. Here the poet watches "six long-headed jazzers play" and notes how a lady of the evening "whose eyes are bold" lifts "high a dress of silken gold." But the poet also is aware, as Arthur Davis points out in "The Harlem of Langston Hughes' Poetry," (*Phylon*, 1952), that amid the noise, joy, and glitter there are "overtones of weariness and despair." After every night of pleasure Harlem must face a gray dawn of disillusionment. In *Fine Clothes to the Jew* the perception of Harlem is a little different. Using the many voices of the black community's unsung, unheroic, and unknown poor, Hughes speaks to his reader audience through blues poems and very effectively written dramatic monologues. Then in *The Dream-Keeper*, the poetry volume which Hughes wrote primarily for children, Harlem becomes the place where young blacks can dream about a future that is bright with hope and about a country that is full of promise for all of its citizens. By 1942, the year of *Shakespeare in Harlem*, the Harlem that was the background for Hughes's "dream-keeper" or the Harlem of jazz, fun, and easy humor of the 1920s was gone forever. Accordingly, the poetry of *One-Way Ticket, Montage, Ask Your Mama*, and many occasional poems written after 1940 reveal a Harlem shorn of its glitter and luster.

It is true, humor lurks in the alleys and byways of the city, and the occasional tinkle of black laughter filters through the clutter and gloom of a city where, for so many, dreams are deferred and hopes annulled.

It was this Harlem that the poet described in an article in *Freedomways* in the summer of 1963:

> Harlem of honey and chocolate and rum and vinegar and lemon and lime and gall. . . . Dusky dream Harlem rumbling into a nightmare tunnel where the subway . . . keeps right on downtown.

Nevertheless, Harlem remained for Hughes a home and a microcosm of black America—the place where the black life-style had its most distinctive authenticity, a place where there were long, colorful parades, midnight knifings, and early-morning shootings. Here one could find street-corner humor, two-timing pimps, and all of the human wear-and-tear that creates a ghetto.

From such a Harlem Langston Hughes sought no escape. Here he wrote hundreds of poems which in myriad ways mirrored Harlem's defeat, disillusionment, and despair. Here he attuned his ear to the gross humor of the barroom or to the blues or religious songs of joy that came out of crowded apartments or storefront churches. And here he came to know, along with the rest of Harlem's citizens, that there is a "certain amount of nothing in a dream deferred." But he also knew that as a poet he was the "dream-keeper," the one charged to make dreams come true—the one charged to forge new beginnings and make "America be America again." He therefore remained in Harlem even after it had become a slum, full of crime and the social blight of the deluded and the depressed. Until his death on May 22, 1967, he lived at number 20, 127th Street, in the only house on the block with ivy growing in the small front yard. By this time most of Harlem's famed writers or entertainers had died or dispersed and, in many instances, were forgotten by all but a faithful few. But the persons that Hughes created—the Madam Johnsons, the Simples, the hard-luckers, and down-and-outers—remained to remind one that a writer for all seasons had once lived and worked in America's largest black ghetto.

References

Davis, Arthur
1952. "The Harlem of Langston Hughes' Poetry," *Phylon* Winter, pp. 276–83.
Ellison, Ralph
1940. "Review of *The Big Sea*," *New Masses* Oct., pp. 231–32.
Locke, Alain
1941. "Of Native Sons: Real and Otherwise," *Opportunity* Jan., pp. 4–9.
Matheus, John F.
1968. "Langston Hughes as Translator," *CLA Journal* June, pp. 319–30.
O'Daniel, Therman
1968. "A Selected Classified Bibliography," *CLA Journal* June, pp. 349–66.
Redding, Saunders
1956. "Review of *I Wonder as I Wander*," *New York Herald Tribune* Dec. 23, p. 6.
Staples, Elizabeth
1959. "Langston Hughes: Malevolent Force," *American Mercury* Jan., pp. 46–50.
Wagner, Jean
1962. *Les Poètes Négres des États-Unis*. Paris: Librairie Ista.
Wright, Richard
1940. [review] *New Republic* Oct. 28, pp. 600–1.

CHAPTER 2

Blues, Jazz, and Low-down Folks

The decade of the 1920s saw Langston Hughes come of age poetically. Not only did he publish his first poem in a major publication, but he also published two books of poetry, *The Weary Blues* (1926) and *Fine Clothes to the Jew* (1927), and won *Opportunity* magazine's poetry prize for his poem "The Weary Blues" in 1925. The year 1926 also saw the publication in the *Nation* of his first major literary essay, "The Negro Artist and the Racial Mountain."

But if these were years of achievement, they were also years of challenge and change. For between 1921, the year in which Hughes at age nineteen published "The Negro Speaks of Rivers" in the *Crisis*, and 1926, the year of the publication of his first book of poems, he fell from critical grace as far as the major black literary spokesmen were concerned. Favored and praised by Harlem's literary elite in 1921, Hughes was, by 1930, virtually a literary persona non grata in certain cultural and literary circles. The principal reason for his quick demise in critical esteem and reputation was his celebration of cabaret life and his less-than-casual preoccupation with blues and jazz. His "Negro Speaks of Rivers" had given no hint that the young poet's literary concerns would shift in that direction so quickly. For, to the arbiters of Negro literary culture, "The Negro Speaks of Rivers" held forth the promise that Hughes would have the kind of literary career that would blend in very well with Negro upper middle-class values. Not only does the poem give the earth's black and brown and beige people a creditable historical past but links them with the dawn and progress of civilization:

> I've known rivers:
> I've known rivers ancient as the world and older than the
> flow of human blood in human veins.

My soul has grown deep like the rivers.

I bathed in the Euphrates when dawns were young.
I built my hut near the Congo and it lulled me to sleep.
I looked upon the Nile and raised the pyramids above it.
I heard the singing on the Mississippi when Abe Lincoln
    went down to New Orleans, and I've seen its muddy
    bosom turn all golden in the sunset.

I've known rivers
Ancient, dusky rivers.

My soul has grown deep like the rivers.

These lines are not only racially edifying but reflect what critic Jean Wagner calls a "racial romanticism" that is pleasantly instructive in the best Horatian sense. Moreover, there are no painful racial or social specifics in the poem to remind one of centuries of racial injustice. Instead, the black man's collective soul is as deep as the collective depth of all of the rivers of history. And too, the young poet, through his naming of Africa's major rivers, establishes a link with the American black man's romantic motherland. Indeed, the poem is a preeminently acceptable statement.

However, by 1925 this same young poet, four years older and more widely travelled and much more attuned to current literary and cultural trends, had changed his poetic style and subject matter. His prizewinning poem "The Weary Blues" provides prima facie evidence that Hughes was no longer staring at distant vistas and contemplating "ancient, dusky rivers." Rather, there is abundant evidence that by 1926 he was beginning to focus on scenes and settings and themes that were less than palatable to the self-appointed monitors of black cultural development during the twenties. In the latter poem, for instance, the scene is not the rivers that gave birth to ancient civilizations but an after-hours club hazy with smoke and filled with the tantalizing tinkle and blues beat of a piano-playing man. According to the young poet it was music that could only come "from a black man's soul":

Droning a drowsy syncopated tune,
Rocking back and forth to a mellow croon,
    I heard a Negro play.
Down on Lenox Avenue the other night
By the pale dull pallor of an old gas light
    He did a lazy sway. . . .

He did a lazy sway....
To the tune o' those Weary Blues.
With his ebony hands on each ivory key
He made that poor piano moan with melody.
O Blues!
Swaying to and fro on his rickety stool
He played that sad raggedy tune like a musical fool.
Sweet Blues
Coming from a black man's soul.

In retrospect, it is now clear that the changes which affected Hughes's poetic manner and matter and general literary attitude were inevitable and irresistible. First, as Nathan Huggins has ably demonstrated in his fine critical study *Harlem Renaissance* (1971), naturalism greatly influenced all American literary expression in the 1920s, and black Harlem was no exception. Moreover, Huggins offers the highly probable argument that some of America's then reigning literary critics believed that, if American literature were to have a significant rebirth, the newly emerging coterie of black writers would have to lead the way. After all, they had a great abundance of primitivistic energy and knew how to "shuffle off" the mortal coils that were stifling creativity in art and literature. Carl Van Doren (*Opportunity*, 1924) was explicit about the anticipated role black authors would play:

What American literature decidedly needs at the moment is color, music, gusto. . . . If the Negroes are not in a position to contribute these items, I do not know what Americans are.

No one endorsed this point of view with greater enthusiasm and esprit than Carl Van Vechten, who, in the words of Nathan Huggins, was the "undisputed prince" of all white literary figures associated with black Harlem in the 1920s. In his article "Our Negro Intellectuals," in the *Crisis* (Aug. 1928), Allison Davis confirmed this assessment in his charge that it was the nefarious, invidious, and sinister influence of Van Vechten that led many black writers astray and brought "Black literary primitivism to its complete fruition." Van Vechten's own fiction proves that he was interested in primitivism; but, as Huggins points out in his evaluation of Van Vechten's importance to the Harlem Renaissance, the latter's own fiction—*Blind Bow-Boy* (1923), *Firecrackers* (1925), *Nigger Heaven* (1926), and *Parties* (1930)—places great stress on "intensification of experience for its own sake" which, in Huggins's opinion, reflected a Wildean "*fin de siecle* decadence." In other words,

Van Vechten believed in the unfettered freedom of the artist or writer to explore all the ranges of human experience. He apparently made no naturalistic assumptions that the artist had to stress ugliness, weakness, dissolution, disorder, or a self-demeaning determinism. As indicated in the preceding chapter, however, certain young black writers like Hughes believed in and practiced naturalism in their poetry and fiction, much to the consternation of "talented tenth" writers and critics like Countee Cullen who were seemingly intrigued by a Victorian view of art and literature. But these are relatively esoteric concerns when compared with other developments which in the early 1920s were having a direct influence on young black writers like Hughes. Because these developments emanated from the black masses, critics of the "talented tenth" persuasion either feigned a blissful unawareness of the importance of these trends or failed to understand that what the "low-down" folk were singing and saying could be grist for the black writer's mill.

One important development in post-World War I America was jazz music—so much a cultural artifact of the twenties that F. Scott Fitzgerald labelled the gin-popping, Charleston-dancing decade "The Jazz Age." Before World War I, jazz music had been only a bawling infant in New Orleans's Storyville—an infant that somehow crawled its way along the Gulf Coast and up the Mississippi River to St. Louis and Chicago. At first, it was Ferdinand "Jelly Roll" Morton, as early as 1902, playing his "Jelly Roll Blues" and other teasing overtures to commercial sex in Storyville's whorehouses, thus giving the word "jazz" its initial, somewhat pejorative meaning. Then, in 1914, Emmanuel Perez' Creole Band came up from New Orleans to open at Chicago's Grand Theater at Thirty-first and State. By the end of World War I, another New Orleans musician, Freddie Keppard, had brought his band to New York. And when Louis Armstrong, in 1922, came from Chicago to New York to join Fletcher Henderson's new big band, jazz had finally become a lusty adult.

What impressed Langston Hughes and others who were sensitive to black folk movements is that this new mode of music came out of the black experience. Admittedly, in the early twenties there were no neat socio-anthropological explanations of origin, source, and cause. All that anyone knew was that jazz had started in New Orleans and that its stress on polyrhythmic drum beats and instrumental improvisation somehow reflected the music of the Congo Square dances at which black New Orleans—slave and free—had shouted, stomped, and danced at regular intervals from 1817 to 1885. Both Eileen Southern in her *The Music of Black Americans*

(1971) and Marshall W. Stearns in his *The Story of Jazz* (1958) state that the cultural additives that helped jazz music get started were the introduction of European instruments and the tradition of the New Orleans funeral march, originally a joyous salute accorded a deceased brother or sister by one of the city's many secret societies.

Another cultural development that influenced Langston Hughes and his youthful contemporaries was the blues. Like jazz, it was rooted in the black experience and emerged as a mode of folk expression during the post-Reconstruction period. Although its four-line stanza in twelve bars, rhyming *aaba*, reminds one of the folk ballads of western Europe, the call and response pattern, the falsetto "holla," and the flatted fifths and sevenths suggest a distant African origin. Apparently, the blues were born of the hard times of slavery but reached their broadest development right after slavery when the burden of individual responsibility in secular and worldly matters became too much for new freedmen to bear. Loneliness, frustration, the victimization of the powerless, and the vicissitudes of love were often the themes of the blues singer. Young men like Langston Hughes found the blues attractive because it was the kind of music that demonstrated the black man's emotional resiliency and his knack for singing his way through personal catastrophe. There is no evidence that the young poet ever heard Ma Rainey sing the blues with her touring Rabbit Foot Minstrels, but the title of Hughes's prizewinning poem "The Weary Blues" suggests that he had probably heard Bessie Smith sing her version of "The Weary Blues" which she had introduced in 1915 in Atlanta's famed 81 Theater. Certainly, Hughes was one of the 100,000 persons who bought a copy of Mamie Smith's recording of "Crazy Blues"—the first known Columbia race record which the celebrated song stylist cut on August 10, 1920.

A third cultural development which affected black literary expression in the twenties was an interest in Africa as the political motherland and symbol of a purifying primitivism. Marcus Garvey's United Negro Improvement Association led the way in exploring a political return to Africa for black Americans; and, although opposed by Du Bois and his "talented tenth" cohorts, the articulate Jamaican captivated the minds of the black masses with his oratory and vision. Similarly, Alain Locke, the artist Aaron Douglas, and others led the way in exploring the esthetic meaning of Africa in the masterpiece of anthologies, *The New Negro*, published in 1925. Not only were the pages of this work festooned with African drawings, but in Alain Locke's essay on "The Legacy of the Ancestral Arts," he explores the "vital connection" between the African artistic idiom and that of the American Negro. In the art of both there was, in Locke's opinion, an emphasis on the "decorative and purely symbolic material."

There is bountiful evidence that the early poetry of Langston Hughes was influenced by all three cultural developments—jazz, blues, and Africa as political refuge and artistic symbol. As has been indicated above, for his concentration on the themes of jazz and blues, he was severely castigated by most of the reigning Negro critics of the day. In the main, these critics assessed culture and the arts from a "talented tenth" perspective; apparently their objective was the development of Negro art forms that would pave the way for full integration into the mainstream of American society. It is interesting to note in this context that the Negro spiritual, in the critics' view, was just such an acceptable art form; blues and jazz were not. The latter were the products of low-down folk who spoke a shamefully ungrammatical dialect, worked hard, and washed little; the spirituals, on the other hand, were the product of the blending of the songful religious zeal of slaves with protestant hymnody. Not only did the Negro spiritual bring color and excitement and anthropomorphic intensity to an often colorless Judeo-Christian religion, but the music of the spirituals bore proof of the enduring creativity of "Black and Unknown Bards of Long Ago." Du Bois had written approvingly of the spirituals in his chapter on the "Sorrow Songs" in *Souls of Black Folk* in 1903, and his endorsement was the best kind of imprimatur. Then, in 1916, Harry T. Burleigh, the organist at New York's ultra-fashionable St. George's Episcopal Church, brought out his *Jubilee Songs of the United States*, with every spiritual musically arranged so that a concert singer could sing it "in the manner of an art song." By the time James Weldon Johnson produced his two *Books of Negro Spirituals* in 1925 and 1926, there was no doubt that the Negro folk spiritual had the full sanction of the Negro elite as a dignified and racially ennobling form of artistic expression.

Countee Cullen, Langston Hughes's fellow poet, was the first to raise a question about the jazz poems in *The Weary Blues*. In his review in *Opportunity* (Feb. 1926), Cullen began by stating that Hughes is "a poet with whom to reckon, to experience, and here and there . . . to quarrel." He conceded that the poems in *The Weary Blues* have about them an air of "utter spontaneity." But the poet, in Cullen's view, was "too much himself." *The Weary Blues* would have been a better volume of poetry had "Mr. Hughes held himself a bit in check," particularly with regard to the jazz poems at the beginning of the volume. Wrote Countee Cullen:

I regard these jazz poems as interlopers in the company of the truly beautiful poems in other sections of the book. . . . I wonder if jazz poems really belong to that dignified company, that select and austere circle of high literary expression which we call poetry.

Cullen was particularly upset by "The Cat and the Saxophone," an experimental poem in which two lovers converse against a background of cabaret music. Unfortunately, the lovers are not "talented tenth" types; they drink corn liquor, make verbal love in public, and end up dancing the Charleston, the famous dance initially popularized in 1922 in Miller and Lyles's musical show *Runnin' Wild*. The background tune is "Everybody Loves My Baby, But My Baby Don't Love Nobody But Me."

> EVERYBODY
> Half-pint—
> Gin?
> No, make it
> LOVES MY BABY
> corn. You like
> liquor
> don't you, honey?
> BUT MY BABY
> Sure. Kiss me,
> DON'T LOVE NOBODY
> daddy.
> BUT ME.

Echoing Jeffrey's famous critical comment on Wordsworth's *Excursion*, Countee Cullen wrote of this poem: "I cannot say, *This will never do*, but I feel that it ought never to have been done." Cullen concluded that, although *The Weary Blues* was effective in spots, Hughes emerged as too much of a "racial artist" and his work reflected "too much emphasis . . . on strictly Negro themes," thus lacking universality of appeal.

Only one other reviewer was considerably more positive. At best, a few shared Cullen's assessment. Jessie Fauset, writing in the *Crisis* (Mar. 1926), hailed Langston Hughes as a "citizen of the world" who had a gift for writing "more tenderly, more understandingly, more humorously" of life in Harlem than any other poet on the contemporary scene. In her view, his poem beginning "Does a jazz band ever sob?" perfectly "epitomized the essence" of Harlem cabaret nightlife. Quite understandably, she lavished considerable praise on "The Negro Speaks of Rivers," thereby seeming to imply some lack of enthusiasm for the jazz poems in the volume. Two other reviewers—DuBose Heyward in the *New York Herald Tribune* (Aug. 1, 1926) and an unknown reviewer in the London *Times Literary Supplement* (July 29, 1926)—were conspicuously silent about the jazz poems. Both hailed Langston Hughes as a valuable new poetical talent, with Heyward regretting that the young Negro tended to confuse "art with social propaganda" and the *Times* reviewer regretting that Hughes seemed to feel "caged" in western civilization.

The dialogue about the artistic merit of Hughes's new poetic style and his concentration on jazz and blues was continued by the poet himself when he published an essay entitled "The Negro Artist and the Racial Mountain" in the *Nation* in June 1926. Ostensibly a solicited response to George Schuyler's "The Negro Art-Hokum," which the *Nation* (May 1926) had published the week before, Hughes's article developed into a long, credal statement which bristled with defensive comments on the inadequacies of the "talented tenth" view of Negro art and culture. The principal point of Schuyler's article to which Hughes was asked to respond was that there were basically no differences between white art and culture and black art and culture. In his somewhat caustic and flippant manner, Schuyler had written: "Aside from his color . . . your Aframerican is merely a lampblacked Anglo-Saxon." Hence the assertion that the black man's art was peculiar or different was to be, in Schuyler's view, "rejected with a loud guffaw by intelligent people." At the beginning of his article, Hughes dismissed Schuyler's contention with dispatch. There was, in truth, a distinct Negro spirit. Not only was the "urge for whiteness" a very high mountain standing in the way of the development of " 'true Negro art,' " but "Nordic faces, Nordic art, and an Episcopal heaven" seem unfortunately to be the primary concerns of upper- and middle-class Negroes who, like Schuyler, would "ape things white." Then Hughes discussed the dilemma of a Negro artist who, like Jean Toomer, was caught between the white critic's demand for racial stereotypes and the black critic's demand for "respectable" plots, settings, and characters. The rest of the article was devoted to a well-articulated defense of the substance and style of his own poetry. In apparent response to Countee Cullen's comment that *The Weary Blues* was too racial and too jazz-oriented, Hughes asserted that his poetry was intentionally "racial in theme and treatment" and by deliberate design reflected "some of the meanings and rhythms of jazz." Jazz, he declared, was

> One of the inherent expressions of Negro life in America: the
> eternal tom-tom beating in the Negro soul—the tom-tom of
> revolt against weariness in a white world . . . the tom-tom of
> joy and laughter, and pain swallowed with a smile.

In reality, Hughes continued, Negro jazz was the product and the
property of the "low-down folks" ("and they are in the majority—
may the Lord be praised!"). If the "smug Negro middle class"
could only turn away from the "white, respectable, ordinary books,
and papers" and savor the joy and ecstasy of low-down folks, its
members would be able to "catch a glimmer" of their own racial
beauty. In conclusion, Hughes promised, with the somewhat abra-
sive bravado of youth, that young artists like himself would continue to "express our dark-skinned selves without fear or shame"
and fully exploit the Negro's experience in all dimensions, regardless
of white or black censure or praise.

Hughes's statement in the *Nation* had a Janus-like significance.
It was not only a vigorous response to Cullen's less-than-laudatory
review of *The Weary Blues*, but it also served as a fitting prelude
to his next volume of poems, *Fine Clothes to the Jew*. The nature of
the poet's self-defense also fixed the boundaries of future critical
discussion of his works. From now on, the subject matter of his
poetry and not the art of his poetry would be the center of the
swirling controversy over his merit as a poet. Indeed, many years
were to elapse before there was sound critical comment on how
Langston Hughes handled language and imagery or before there
was an assessment of the esthetic quality of his work. During the
twenties no one seemed to be interested in evaluating his technical
craftsmanship as a poet. No one wondered what effect his self-pro-
claimed mode of spontaneous poetic composition had on his poetic
form. His major critics were race and culture specialists who were
quite incapable of assessing the finer qualities of his poetry.

In this context it is appropriate to add that the critical controversy
swirled around his use of jazz and blues and low-life incidents as
poetic subject matter. No one discussed the merit of his many poems
on Africa. Indeed, such a critical discussion had to wait until 1962
when Jean Wagner published his *Les Poètes Nègres des États-Unis*
and commented extensively on the "African atavism" in Langston
Hughes's early poetry. As mentioned earlier, there was widespread
interest among Harlem's intellectuals in Africa both as artistic symbol and political refuge. We now know that given the cultural
climate of the 1920s Hughes was right on target with his Africa
poems. When he wrote of "World-wide dusk/Of dear dark faces/

Driven before an alien wind," he gave in summary the long tedious
history of the African diaspora. And when he wrote:

> All the tom-toms of the jungle beat in my blood
> And all the wild hot moons of the jungles shine in my soul.
> I am afraid of this civilization—

he was poetizing the message of Marcus Garvey, who had spoken
of such fear and such hope to the members of the United Negro
Improvement Association. Hughes retained a continuing concern
for Africa right up to the time of his death, and it is unfortunate
that during the twenties critics tended to ignore this aspect of his
poetical contribution.

At the end of "The Negro Artist and the Racial Mountain"
Hughes promised to build a poetical temple for tomorrow and de-
vote his talent to "racial-self-expression without fear or shame."
This he did in his second volume of poetry, *Fine Clothes to the Jew*.
The effect on spokesmen for the middle and upper classes of Negro
society was something akin to mass apoplexy. The critical review
of the work in the *Pittsburgh Courier* was headlined "Langston
Hughes' Book of Poems Trash," and that in the *Amsterdam News*
"Langston Hughes—The Sewer Dweller." Chicago's Negro paper
the *Whip* called Hughes "The poet lowrate of Harlem," and Eustace Gay of the *Philadelphia Tribune* wrote (1927):

> It does not matter to me whether every poem in the book is
> true to life. Why should it be paraded before the American
> public by a Negro author as being typical or representative of
> the Negro? Bad enough to have white authors holding up our
> imperfections to public gaze. Our aim ought to be to present
> to the general public . . . our higher aims and aspirations.

What were the fierce improprieties of *Fine Clothes to the Jew*
which provoked this furor? The simple fact was that about one-
third of the poems in the volume were in form and fact blues poems
and the balance were blues in spirit, if not in form. One example is
the poem "Hard Luck" from which the volume received its title:

> When hard luck overtakes you
> Nothin' for you to do.
> When hard luck overtakes you
> Nothin' for you to do.
> Gather up your fine clothes
> An' sell 'em to de Jew.

Jew takes yo' fine clothes,
Gives you a dollar an' a half.
Jew takes yo' fine clothes,
Gives you a dollar an' a half.
Go to de bootleg's,
Git some gin to make you laugh.

This poem's celebration of the casual hedonism of the urban Negro embarrassed the Negro race's ambassadors of culture and refinement. How could they instill the proper attitudes toward the puritan work ethic when poets like Langston Hughes were singing the joys of economic improvidence? But if they were embarrassed by a poem like "Hard Luck," they were infuriated by a poem like "Bad Man"—simply because it presented a character who had been stereotyped by white America as a black Saturday-night crime statistic:

I beats ma wife an'
I beats ma side gal too.
Beats ma wife an'
Beats ma side gal too.
Don't know why I do it but
It keeps me from feelin' blue.

The *Crisis* mounted its attack on *Fine Clothes to the Jew* and Negro literature of that "ilk" in the aforementioned article entitled "Our Negro Intellectuals," published in its issue of August 1928. To write the article Du Bois, *Crisis* editor, secured the services of Allison Davis, presently a distinguished social anthropologist and psychologist, but in 1928 a recent product of Williams and Harvard and a literary scholar and critic of impeccable reputation. The objective of the essay was not only to censure, with "learned rebuke," young Negro writers like Hughes and Fisher and McKay, but to end forthwith the diabolical influence of Carl Van Vechten on those writers. Presumably, it was thought at the time that a brilliant Phi Beta Kappa scholar with a master's degree from Harvard could easily decimate Van Vechten, a writer from Iowa who had been wealthy enough to go to Yale. In his initial sentence, Davis arraigned the accused writers as follows:

For nearly ten years, our Negro writers have been "confessing" the distinctive sordidness and triviality of Negro life, and making an exhibition of their own unhealthy imagination, in

the name of frankness and sincerity, of war against hypocrisy.
. . . Sincerity is no defense for the sensationalism of Dr. Rudolph Fisher's *High Yaller* or Mr. Langston Hughes' *Fine Clothes to the Jew.*

Davis then stated that Carl Van Vechten had induced young Negro writers to write about cabaret nightlife in Harlem and about Africa. Not only had Van Vechten's *Nigger Heaven* "warped Negro life into a fantastic barbarism," but this white author had used the preface he wrote to *The Weary Blues* to promote the cause of an "undiluted primitivism." Further, Van Vechten had "misdirected" Mr. Hughes, "a genuine poet who gave promise of a power and technique exceptional in any poetry." Davis did concede, however, that all that was wrong with the poetry of Mr. Hughes could not be placed at Van Vechten's door. The decision to write poetry exploiting "the meretricious themes of jazz" was the poet's own. Also, it was the poet himself who sacrificed "his indubitable gift" to a "dogma" that demanded a poetry that was "atavistic and colorful" but not truly imaginative. In conclusion, Davis expressed regret that Harlem's young writers chose to concentrate upon "immediate and crude emotions" rather than on the "essential Negro qualities of fortitude, irony, and an absence of self-pity."

Langston Hughes was quick to respond to Allison Davis's adverse criticism. In a letter published in the very next issue of the *Crisis,* the poet denied being "misdirected" by Van Vechten. In the first place, he asserted, many of the poems were written before he had made the acquaintance of Van Vechten. In the second place, those written after meeting Van Vechten were "not about him, not requested by him, . . . some of them not liked by him nor . . . do they in any way bear his poetic influence." Flashing the same kind of authorial bravado previously displayed in his "Negro Artist and the Racial Mountain," he declared that, if the poems in *Fine Clothes* were "low down, jazzy, cabaretish, sensational and utterly uncouth in the eyes of Mr. Davis, the fault is mine—not Mr. Van Vechten's." Then, he closed with his now famous statement, so full of pointed innuendo: "I have never pretended to keep a literary grazing pasture with food to suit all breeds of cattle."

Fortunately, during this time *Fine Clothes to the Jew* had some defenders and some enthusiastic advocates. One such was Margaret Larkin, who in a review in *Opportunity* (Mar. 1927) stated that the blues poems of Hughes's second volume of poetry were fraught with social meaning and that it was good to behold the emergence of "a poet for the people." Another critic who defended *Fine*

Clothes was that urbane littérateur, Alain Locke. In a review entitled "Common Clay and Poetry" (*Saturday Review*, Apr. 1927), he hailed the bluesy, low-down poems as proof that Langston Hughes was that kind of rare poetic genius who could "strip life to the buff and poetize it." Indeed, the poems were more than mere poetry—they were "vivid, pulsing, creative portraits of Negro folk foibles and moods." They were full of the "crying laugh that eases misery." They revealed how the "sordidness of common life" could be "caught up in the lilt of poetry." In fact, some of the poems, like "Song for a Dark Girl" and "Mulatto" were so "pregnant with social as well as individual tragedy" that they proved that Hughes possessed a "tragic vision," rare in a poet of his comparative immaturity and inexperience.

Another writer who, in a sense, strode forward to defend Hughes was Charles S. Johnson. In an article entitled "Jazz Poetry and Blues," Johnson provided a "class-action" defense, as it were, of the new breed of Negro writer who had dared to write about the folk of Negro society—the "cabaret singers, porters, street walkers, elevator boys . . . hard luck victims . . . sinners, and hard working men." Interestingly enough, Johnson, who was the first editor of *Opportunity* magazine and went on to become a top-rated sociologist and ultimately president of Fisk University, published his essay in the *Carolina Magazine* (May 1928)—a fact suggesting that the Chapel Hill publication was experiencing in 1928 a kind of creeping literary liberalism from which *Crisis* of the NAACP was temporarily immune. Also, it should be noted that Johnson's observations and comments indicate a quality of literary perceptivity not often found in sociologists who become university presidents. He wrote:

> The new racial poetry of the Negro is the expression of something more than experimentation in a new technique. It marks the birth of a new racial consciousness and self-conception. It is a first frank acceptance of race, and the recognition of difference without the usual implications of disparity. It lacks apology, the wearying appeals to pity, and the conscious philosophy of defense. In being itself it reveals its greatest charm. In accepting this life it invests it with a new meaning. "The Negro" of popular conception is not the educated person of Negro blood; he is the peasant, the dull, dark worker, or shirker of work, who sprawls his shadow over the South and clutters the side streets of northern cities. These are the forgotten lives that thread about within their circles, who run the full scale of human emotions without being suspected of feeling.

... He who would know something about the core and limitations of this life should go to the Blues. In them is the curious story of disillusionment without a saving philosophy and yet without defeat. They mark these narrow limits of life's satisfactions, its vast treacheries and ironies. Stark, full human passions crowd themselves into an uncomplex expression, so simple in their power that they startle. If they did not reveal a fundamental and universal emotion of the human heart, they would not be noticed now as the boisterous and persistent intruders in the society of lyrics that they are.

For its time, and considering the intense intraracial discussions then taking place regarding appropriate approaches to Negro literature, Charles S. Johnson's essay is remarkably prophetic. Certainly, it is an effective companion statement to Langston Hughes's bold announcement, two years earlier, that as a poet he would explore racial self-expression "without fear or shame," relating both how "the tom-tom cries" and "laughs" and somehow capturing in poetry the incredible mixture of beauty and ugliness in the black experience in America, in Africa, and on the islands of the sea.

Inevitably, with the passing of time, tensions have subsided, perspectives broadened, and critics have become more understanding of what Langston Hughes was trying to do with blues and jazz in his early poetry. Certainly, whatever "talented tenth" opposition there was to Hughes's blues and jazz poetry practically evaporated during the depression-ridden 1930s and the war-torn 1940s, with one or two exceptions which will be noted below. By 1945, even the most avid "talented tenth" advocate had begun to realize that racial integration was a political problem and not a cultural or social problem; close observance of the cultural and social amenities of the larger society could not earn a black man his civil rights. Concomitantly, by the 1940s there was a new climate of acceptance of black folk literature and art on all black social levels.

Proof of a change of mood and of attitude is found in Arna Bontemps assessment of Hughes in his article "The Harlem Renaissance" in the *Saturday Review* (Mar. 1947). In Bontemps's eyes, Hughes is not a low-down blues writer and purveyor of racially shameful material but a superb "chronicler of modern urbanization" and a "singer with an ear for street music and folk idioms." The appearance of other works of literature by blacks helped to create this new climate of acceptance. First, there was the enormously popular novel *Native Son* by Richard Wright, which showed how deferred dreams in Chicago's south side ghetto could lead to crime and murder. Similarly, Gwendolyn Brooks's poems in *A Street in Bronzeville* (1945) dealt forthrightly with ghetto frustrations and disappointments and showed how the problems of the urban black ghetto in American cities had become increasingly obvious. As a consequence, the blues and jazz poetry of Hughes acquired an even greater significance and relevance. Some ten years earlier, Benjamin Brawley in *The Negro Genius* (1937) had expressed his deep and abiding regret that *Fine Clothes to the Jew* had ever been published, for its poems reflected "the abandon and vulgarity" of the twenties. But Sterling Brown, in his review of Brawley's book in *Opportunity* (Sept. 1937), ably defended Hughes's work and expressed his own regret about Brawley's rigidly Victorian approach to life and literature.

Further proof that the critical climate was improving was the appearance of Arthur Davis's very perceptive essay "The Harlem of Langston Hughes' Poetry," *Phylon* (1952). Davis notes that in Hughes's poems on Harlem there is a note of gay abandon, but there is also a note of urban weariness. Sometimes the dancing and the merrymaking become a little desperate and frenetic. For this reason, if one listens closely, one can hear "a jazz band sob" in the early morning hours. Davis's conclusion is that even in his early salutes to "Jazzonia," city of jazz, Hughes's poetry contains an undercurrent of tension and misery. The best jazz music is a tune "That laughs and cries at the same time." Indeed, Hughes's players and laughers and jazz buffs are all like his "Jester":

> Because my mouth
> Is wide with laughter
> You do not hear
> My inner cry?
> Because my feet
> Are gay with dancing
> You do not know I die.

The implications of Davis's approach to Hughes's Harlem poetry suggest two conclusions: first, the poet was more than a facile versifier dealing only in matters of surface social significance and, second, Hughes apparently knew that Harlem had a deferred dream that might explode even when he was watching Midnight Nan do her dance at LeRoy's in the mid-twenties.

The most extensive critical assessment of Hughes's poetry for all periods of his writing career is found in Jean Wagner's *Black Poets of the United States* (1973). Published originally in French as *Les*

Poètes Négres des États Unis (1962), the text was translated into
English by Kenneth Douglas, thus providing scholars in Afro-
American literature with a critical study of major Negro poets from
Dunbar through Sterling Brown. Wagner's study of Hughes is
thorough, delving into every aspect of the poet's career; but, at the
outset, the critic makes several generalizations that in a sense suggest
a bias on his part that could militate against his providing a fair and
judicious assessment of the poet's work. He finds four weaknesses
in his poetry (p. 386):

> A sometimes excessive facility, an impulsiveness not always
> restrained by a judicious rein, a too frequent uncalled-for vul-
> garity for its own sake, and on occasion, the cultivation of
> originality at any price. . . .

These weaknesses, Wagner argues, "do not diminish the intrinsic
worth" of the poet's achievement as the "most productive poet of
the Negro Renaissance," but there is no doubt that they becloud the
critic's judgment. One suspects that this general initial assessment
of Hughes was motivated by the Harlem poet's failure to approxi-
mate in function or attitude or role what Wagner considered to be
proper for the poet in Western society. Hughes was not, for instance, a fiery rebel who, standing on the hills of a superior wisdom,
hurled diatribes of verse down on the erring urban masses. He was
more of a spokesman and an interpreter for those masses and not
enough of a gadfly critic and social irritant. Then too, self-torturing
inner tensions were absent in Hughes; indeed, he appeared to be too
easygoing and too well adjusted to be a genuine poet. His was no
tortured genius, pitted against a massively hostile world; he did not
burn enough with disenchantment. He was not a ferociously mal-
adjusted, angry man. Nor was he a heroic loner or philosophic iso-
late. Actually, Hughes was a perapatetic cosmopolite—a man who
made his convivial way to all shores and way stations and seemingly
had more friends than enemies. One suspects that, given this kind
of man, Wagner felt that the effervescent, well-adjusted Harlemite
could not be the kind of poet the French critic admired.

Wagner also demonstrates an inability to comprehend all of the
far-flung implications of living in a black urban ghetto. For instance,
he belabors what he considers to be a significant difference between
the urban "masses" and the "folk" (p. 394):

> The folk have roots, ties to the earth, while the masses whose
> joys and sorrows, both material and moral, are depicted by

Hughes in the sometimes shocking hues of the naturalist pal-
ette, and with whom his own origins ensured obvious affinities,
for the most part are flotsam, uprooted human beings as yet
ill-fitted for the harsh, unfamiliar urban environment to which
the barriers of segregation and the economic necessities of the
epoch had driven them.

Needless to say, such a distinction is unnecessary in black America
where the "uprooted" who fled to the cities had once been "folk"
who had been too well tied to the earth. Because he makes this unnecessary distinction, however, Wagner fails to understand and
evaluate Hughes's self-assigned poetic role as one obligated to record, in infinite poetic detail, how erstwhile rural folk adjusted and
survived as semisophisticated urbanites in an America that was
basically hostile to their race and kind.

Despite these limitations in critical orientation, Wagner labors to
present a full poetic profile of Langston Hughes. Particularly does
he make a total effort to discuss all of the implications of the poet's
involvement with, and use of, jazz. In a section entitled "Rebellion: Through a Glass Jazzily," Wagner undertakes to show that
Hughes's use of jazz was initially a mode of rebellion—"the tom-
tom of revolt against weariness in a white world," as the poet himself had stated in his "Negro Artist and the Racial Mountain." But
in his poetry, jazz is more than a means of rebellion; according to
the poet: "The rhythm of life/Is a jazz rhythm." Jazz is the substance of life itself. From the "talented tenth" perspective the celebration of jazz was a mode of rebellion against the somewhat prudish
bourgeois standards of racial self-improvement; but, in actuality,
jazz was a way of life enveloping both white and black America.
Wagner is on safer ground when he asserts that jazz in Hughes's
poetry is a means of escape from the boring routine of getting and
spending in a highly competitive urban environment. Even so, one
must quibble with his language when he writes (pp. 404-5):

> jazz . . . is a means of escape, another kind of addiction whose
> artificial paradises the poet equates with those obtained by the
> intravenous injection of a narcotic. For the popular masses in
> those immense ghettoes . . . the temple of jazz, the nightclub,
> is also the sanctuary of an illusion, where floodlights replace
> moonlight and the sea's swaying immensity shrinks to the
> dimensions of a few sips of liquor from a shot glass.

This seems to be a verbal overreaction to Hughes's use of the jazz-
as-escape theme.

Wagner also sees in the poet's use of jazz a plea for the "Negro's *carpe diem*: . . . Tomorrow . . . who knows?/Dance today!" And he notes the point, made so forcefully by Arthur Davis, that "the sound of jazz always has an admixture of despair." But Wagner carries this critical argument a step further and states that the Negro's use of jazz is another mode of mask-wearing and is thus linked to Dunbar's poem "We Wear the Mask." Here one wonders if the French critic has not confused sheer urban fatigue with the black man's ancient need for guile and deception in times of racial conflict. Wagner also sees in Hughes's use of jazz a definable "erotic content." He notes that in one poem "the insidious rhythms of jazz are accompanied by the erotic convolutions of the naked black dancing girl. . . ." In a sense, this is the kind of "talented tenth" observation that would have delighted a Benjamin Brawley, who viewed the jazz age as one of "abandon and vulgarity." Actually, dancing has always been an art form, and art and eros were associated long before the discovery of jazz. Moreover, there is evidence of some critical misreading of the poem in question; there may be some "erotic convolutions," but the girl in the poem is not naked or, at least, evidence of her nakedness is lacking:

> Wine-maiden
> Of the jazz-tune night,
> Lips
> Sweet as purple dew
> Breasts
> Like the pillows of all sweet dreams,
> Who crushed
> The grapes of joy
> And dripped their juice
> On you?

As Blyden Jackson very wisely points out in his comments on Hughes in *Black Poetry in America* (1974), Langston Hughes's poetry is a mélange of sharply noted spontaneous impressions gathered from the black urban scene. These impressions, communicated with a technical skill often obscured by the poet's mask of casual creativity, in turn provoke equally sharp reader reactions or impressions. In these lines, Hughes is provocative and suggestive, and it is difficult for a reader like Wagner not to strip this "Midnight Dancer" who has been anointed by the crushed juice of the "grapes of joy."

Wagner also recognizes that jazz not only affected the content

of Hughes's poetry but affected his poetic technique as well. Unlike
Countee Cullen, who questioned whether "The Cat and the Saxophone" was poetry, the French critic sees the poem as an effective
technical experiment "neither more nor less blameworthy than some
of E. E. Cummings's and Guillaume Apollinaire's experiments, and
with these it must no doubt be grouped."

Finally, Wagner views Hughes's use of jazz as a forthright expression of Negro primitivism, and in this observation he finds full
support in the poetry. Jazz was "Harlem's heartbeat." The critic
writes (p. 403):

> The actual substance of jazz is Negro life, especially that of
> the great black metropolis. Between Harlem's heartbeats and
> the beat of the rhythm section . . . there are natural affinities. . . .

Wagner's analysis of the poet's use of the blues is presented in
two sections of his criticism, and in both sections he displays some
naiveté about the source and nature of the blues. In the first section,
"The Social Setting of the Blues," effective analysis of the blues
poetry is blocked by the intrusion of a lengthy, somewhat intense
discussion of how and why Hughes tended to associate evil and
trouble with black skin color. Admittedly, Wagner might not have
known that "Black-is-evil" had long been a sort of in-house racial
joke among American Negroes, but one does wonder why he
would go to some lengths to document a folk belief of this kind.
Also, Wagner is distressed by the low-down nature of Hughes's
blues world. He regrets (p. 425) that it is a

> half-world peopled with unwed mothers and prostitutes,
> pimps, homosexuals and drug addicts, together with drunks,
> gamblers, bad men, and killers.

Here again, Wagner reveals a lack of awareness of the essential folk
origins of the blues in the Afro-American context. Nor does he
appear to understand that in a black urban ghetto this "half-world"
is very often the whole world.

The second section providing comment on the blues in Hughes's
poetry is entitled "Religion and the Masses." After stating that the
poet was not the kind of person who had "those crises of conscience" in religious matters "that seize upon certain delicate souls
and shake them to their very depths," Wagner says that "as the poet
of jazz," Hughes was particularly "well-fitted" to be "the interpreter of the orgiastic religion of black people of the lower classes."

This latter conclusion is based on the critic's assumption that there is a "basic identity of nature and function" between religious exaltation and the exaltation inspired by jazz. In other words, Wagner sees an "identity between the profane and sacred modes of Negro lyric expressivity," and supports this point of view with documentation from the work of ethnomusicologists and jazz critics. Admittedly, this is a provocative assumption. Unfortunately, such an assumption leads Wagner to the erroneous critical conclusion that some of Hughes's religious poems in the "Glory Halleluiah" section of *Fine Clothes to the Jew* are "perfect" religious equivalents of the blues. One example given by Wagner of such a "blues" poem is "Feet o' Jesus":

> At the feet o' Jesus,
> Sorrow like a sea.
> Lordy, let yo' mercy
> Come driftin' down on me.

Langston Hughes may have been an irreligious man who, in Wagner's words, tended to "reduce religious problems to social problems," but the poet would never have confused a religious moan with a blues "holla." In his article "My Adventures as a Social Poet," *Phylon* (1947), Hughes recalled an incident that reminded him of the yawning gulf between the secular and the spiritual which all poets must vigilantly respect. He stated that on one weekday night, when he was reading a poem about hard work and hard luck from the pulpit of an Atlantic City church, he was stopped by a note from the preacher who demanded that he not read "any more blues in my pulpit." Wagner is certainly right in his assertion that Langston Hughes was not, overtly at least, a profoundly religious man. But he is wrong in his assumption that the poet did not know the difference between a blues poem and a religious poem.

Two other writers have made comments on Langston Hughes's use of jazz and blues. One is George Kent, whose observations are to be found in his book *Blackness and the Adventure of Western Culture* (1972). In an essay entitled "Langston Hughes and the Afro-American Folk and Cultural Tradition" he makes several provocative observations bearing on the poet's blues poetry. First, Hughes was a poet who was "full of the folk"—one whose poetry continually explored "the rich density of the folk hope." He was a successful folk artist because he had "an instinctive . . . sense of the folk acceptance of the contradictory as something to be borne." For this reason, Hughes's folk poems and blues contain no resolutions and provide no solutions to life's dilemmas. All that one can do in a Hughes poem full of life's contrarieties is to conclude that life "jes be's that way." Like Arthur Davis, Kent also sees in Hughes's Harlem jazz poetry "increasing desperation and decreasing joy." This critic is most effective and original, however, in his discussion of the "blues devices" used in the poet's blues poetry. These are contrast, wit, folk imagery, and voice tones. Using these devices, Hughes wrote a blues poetry that enabled him to stay tuned in on the black urban experience in all of its dimensions. Kent concludes that some of the poet's best work is that which captures the spirit of the blues but dispenses with the so-called blues devices. In "Lover's Return," for instance, one finds irony, dramatic concreteness, and a folk acceptance of an unresolvable dilemma but none of the specific blues devices:

> My old time daddy
> Came back home last night.
> His face was pale and
> His eyes didn't look just right. . . .
>
> I looked at my daddy—
> Lawd! and I wanted to cry.
> He looked so thin—
> Lawd! that I wanted to cry.
> But the devil told me:
> *Damn a lover*
> *Come home to die!*

Kent and others argue that Hughes lacked the capacity to fashion a work of poetry having "the big vision"; but, as this poem demonstrates, a vignette giving only a small piece of the action is really all one needs to sense the full dimension of an overpowering human dilemma.

Finally, Blyden Jackson in his essay on Langston Hughes in *Black Poetry in America* has made some comments which deserve mention before closing this chapter. First, Jackson agrees with many other critics that Hughes was the master of both the blues form and the "architectonics" of the jazz poem. Three gifts enabled him to do this. First, Hughes had an ear for dialect and developed some mastery of both the dramatic monologue and dialogue as poetic forms (Kent calls these forms "voice tones"). Secondly, he mastered the art of disciplined esthetic detachment from racial trauma. He could create art out of what Kent calls the "contradictory" without, as Jackson says, any "warm wallowing in his own emotions." Third—and this becomes very important in explaining Hughes's success as a jazz poet—he was a great impressionist. Within a few flitting minutes he could verbally capture a scene or poetically editorialize on an incident; and then scene, poet, and incident would be gone, forever lost in the changing chimera of circumstance. The reader receives the poet's impression of

> The Negro
> With the trumpet at his lips
> Has dark moons of weariness
> Beneath his eyes

He hears the "thump, thump, thump" as the jazz pianist pounds out "The Weary Blues" in a smoke-filled room. He sees "six long-headed jazzers." All are flitting impressions captured by the poet; and, as Jackson says, "Impressions tend to lack depth." Moreover, when one puts them together, does one really have the truth or one man's ever-changing impression of the truth? Jackson concludes that Hughes's great weakness was that he could not or did not synthesize his multiple impressions into something big and comprehensive. But one can reply that the age of cabaret jazz of the twenties was a time of swiftly swirling events and dazzling movement. There was no time to put down the entire story, with a beginning, a middle, and an end. There was just time to record bits and pieces of the swiftly passing scene as viewed by one poet. Just as the blues were different for each person at any given time, jazz was somehow different each time it was heard.

Only Langston Hughes, master impressionist, could effectively depict black America's first great period of blues and jazz and low-down folks. Admittedly, his poems on Harlem's jazz age do not provide the reader with a sustained and unified image of the period of the Harlem Renaissance. Rather, one senses the kaleidoscopic variety of the 1920s, much in the sense that McKay's hero, Jake, views Harlem in the novel *Home to Harlem*. As the latter makes his picaresque, joy-seeking way from cabaret to cabaret and from woman to woman, Harlem for him is an ever-shifting scene. And one can imagine that a newly arrived Harlemite would discern the abrupt contrast between the exciting variety of his new city with the enduring monotony of ritual and observance in his former home in the rural South. And, although Hughes's poetic impressions of Harlem connote variety and movement, a certain architectonic unity emerges, tying together "long-headed jazzers," downtown pleasure seekers, happy religionists, hard-drinking sinners, and young and old lovers in the exciting circus that was Harlem of the twenties. As in a circus, one has a panoramic view of a series of exciting events, but one can only attend to the activities in one ring at a time. So it is with Langston Hughes's poetry of Harlem's jazz and blues age. Each impressionistic poetical bit is a small ring in a larger urban circus.

References

Bontemps, Arna
  1947. "The Harlem Renaissance," *Saturday Review of Literature* Mar. 22, pp. 12–13, 44.
Brawley, Benjamin
  1937. *The Negro Genius.* New York: Dodd, Mead.
Brown, Sterling A.
  1937. "Review of *The Negro Genius*," *Opportunity* Sept., pp. 280–81.
Cullen, Countee
  1926. "Review of *The Weary Blues*," *Opportunity* Feb., pp. 73-74.
Davis, Allison
  1928. "Our Negro Intellectuals," *Crisis* Aug., p. 268–69.
Davis, Arthur
  1952. "The Harlem of Langston Hughes' Poetry," *Phylon* 8:276–83.
Fauset, Jessie
  1926. "Review of *The Weary Blues*," *Crisis* Mar., p. 239.
Gay, Eustace
  1927. "Review of *Fine Clothes to the Jew*," *Philadelphia Tribune* Mar. 8, p. 4.
Heyward, DuBose
  1926. "Review of *The Weary Blues*," *New York Herald Tribune* Aug. 1, p. 4.
Hughes, Langston
  1926. "The Negro Artist and the Racial Mountain," *Nation* June, pp. 692–94.
Huggins, Nathan
  1971. *Harlem Renaissance.* New York: Oxford Univ. Pr.
Jackson, Blyden, and Louis Rubin
  1974. *Black Poetry in America.* Baton Rouge: Louisiana State Univ. Pr.
Johnson, Charles S.
  1928. "Jazz Poetry and Blues," *Carolina Magazine* May, pp. 16–20.
Kent, George
  1971. "Langston Hughes and the Afro-American Folk and Cultural Tradition," pp. 53–75. In *Blackness and the Adventure of Western*

Culture. Chicago: Third World Pr.; also in *Langston Hughes: Black Genius*, edited by Therman O'Daniel, pp.182–210. New York: Morrow.

Larkin, Margaret
1927. "A Poet for the People," *Opportunity* Mar., pp. 84–85.

Locke, Alain
1927. "Common Clay and Poetry," *Saturday Review of Literature* Apr., p. 712.

Schuyler, George
1926. "The Negro Art-Hokum," *Nation* May, pp. 662–63.

Southern, Eileen
1971. *The Music of Black Americans*. New York: Norton.

Stearns, Marshall W.
1958. *The Story of Jazz*. New York: Oxford Univ. Pr.

Van Doren, Carl
1924. "The Younger Generation of Negro Writers," *Opportunity* May, p. 145.

Wagner, Jean
1962. *Les Poètes Négres des États-Unis*. Paris: Librairie Ista.

CHAPTER 3

A New Song
for an Old Hurt

As indicated in chapter 1, Hughes produced five volumes of poetry in the 1930s—*Dear Lovely Death, The Dream-Keeper, The Negro Mother, Scottsboro Limited,* and *A New Song.* During this decade he further broadened his literary range and output by publishing a prizewinning novel, *Not Without Laughter* (1930); a volume of short stories, *The Ways of White Folks* (1934); seven full-length and two one-act plays. At least two of his dramatic productions enjoyed the distinction of having long runs: *Mulatto,* a three-act tragedy written in the late twenties, ran on Broadway and on tour for almost twenty months in 1935; *Don't You Want to be Free?,* a long one-act play, set a record of 135 performances at the New York Suitcase Theater in 1937.

Despite the quality and range of Hughes's literary productivity during the 1930s, at least two prominent literary spokesmen issued rather disparaging appraisals of his literary output during this period. The first statement is found in an article, "The Negro and American Culture," by V. F. Calverton in the *Saturday Review of Literature* in 1940. Calverton, an editor in 1929 of an anthology of American Negro literature who zealously supported Negro literary and cultural causes during the so-called "wet-nursing" years of the 1920s, was certainly authorized by experience and interest to comment on the literary career of Langston Hughes. Calverton begins his article by bestowing lavish praise on McKay's *Harlem Shadows* (1922) for its rich "tropicality" and "pagan zeal." Then he dismisses Langston Hughes: "Hughes, it must be admitted has not been idle, but his work has not grown in importance. Rather it has stood still." He concludes by stating the hope that "newer" figures like Wright, Hurston, and Tolson would have "greater staying power and growth" than Hughes. Calverton's last observation is interesting: not only does it indicate that he lacked the gift of prophecy (Hughes in many ways "outstayed" all three of the writers cited by Calverton), but it also shows that one can make a comparison without making a critical judgment.

The second critical assessment of Hughes's literary career in the 1930s is found in Harold Cruse's *The Crisis of the Negro Intellectual.* Originally published in 1967, this somewhat opinionated appraisal of Negro literary, political, and cultural trends and movements in and around New York City has been an enormously popular work (by 1971 it had gone through its fifth printing). Although the book contains little or no literary criticism per se and most of the author's comments on Negro writers are ad hominem (or ad feminem) strictures, whatever critical pronouncements there are are delivered with an almost sledgehammer directness. Of Langston Hughes Cruse writes (p. 307):

> ... Langston Hughes unfortunately ... never developed much in scope beyond the artistic, aesthetic and intellectual limits of the 1920's. He was one of the aborted renaissance men ... a man of culture without a cultural philosophy.

As in Calverton's case, Cruse's critical generalization is not supported by any objective evidence; but their statements, if unchallenged, leave Hughes's literary reputation during the 1930s slowly twisting in the wind of critical disapprobation.

The evidence at hand, both in Dickinson's *Bio-Bibliography* of Langston Hughes (1967) and Therman O'Daniel's "Selected Classified Bibliography" in *Langston Hughes: Black Genius,* 1971, directly disputes the assertions by both Calverton and Cruse that there was no development in Hughes's literary career during the 1930s. Not only had Hughes mastered the new genres of fiction and drama, but as a poet he broadened his range of subject matter, moving beyond the treatment of Harlem's folk types to black folk throughout the African diaspora. Also, as will be seen later in this chapter, he broadened his poetical scope to include leftist issues and causes. Admittedly, to critics who value and emphasize the esthetic estimate in appraising a poet, the broadening of a poet's areas of social and political concern need not constitute development. To this category of critic poetical expression is somehow denigrated if the social and political themes become too important. Unfortunately, this is a problem that many critics have in evaluating the work of writers like Langston Hughes and other black authors whose writings can never be separated from social and political issues. As dramatist Arthur Miller once wrote, however, "The fish is in the water and the water is in the fish." Similarly, the black writer is part of a social and political system which inevitably affects the quality and range of one's literary statement. Thus, when Hughes expanded his literary interests to meet new and different political and social contingencies (the Scottsboro case discussed below is an example), he had to develop new and different literary strategies. Admittedly, these new directions did not meet with the approval of critics like Calverton and Cruse and others who, as we will see later, have charged that Hughes as writer developed little or not at all after his burst of literary output in the 1920s. In the final analysis, however, there is no arguing critical tastes. But even those critics who might loudly affirm "de gustibus non disputandum" ought to document and elucidate their critical positions. This Calverton and Cruse did not do.

One area in which Hughes developed as a poet during the 1930s was in the quality and power of some of the occasional poems published during this time in *Crisis* and *Opportunity*. One such poem is a four-liner called "Today," published in *Opportunity* in October 1937:

> This is earthquake
> Weather:
> Honor and Hunger
> Walk lean together.

The occasional poem, however, which is most important in considering developments in Hughes's literary career during the 1930s is "A New Song." In many respects, it is a credal statement presented to explain new and significant directions in his writing career. Evidently, Hughes deemed the poem to be a very important revelation of his new purpose and insights, for he submitted it to both *Opportunity* and *Crisis*. The former published it in its January 1933 issue and the latter in its issue of March 1933. Cited here are some of the lines which reflect what the editor of *Opportunity* called "a note of defiance hitherto unheard among Negro poets except in the bitter tones of Claude McKay:"

> I speak in the name of the black millions.
> Let all others keep silent a moment.
> I have this word to bring,
> This thing to say
> This song to sing:
>
> > Bitter was the day
> > When I bowed my back

    Beneath the slaver's whip.

That day is past.

    Bitter was the day
    When I saw my children unschooled,
    My young men without a voice in the world,
    My women taken as the body-toys
    Of a thieving people.

That day is past.

    Bitter was the day, I say,
    When the lyncher's rope
    Hung about my neck,
    And the fire scorched at my feet.
    And the white world had no pity,
    And only in the sorrow songs
    Relief was found—
    Yet not relief,
    But merely humble life and silent death
    Eased by a Name
    That hypnotized the pain away—
    O, precious Name of Jesus in that day!

That day is past.

    I know full well now
    Jesus could not die for me—
    That only my own hands
    Dark as the earth,
    Can make my earth-dark body free.
    O, world,
    No longer shall you say
    With arrogant eyes and tall white head:
    "You are my servant,
    Nigger—
    I, the free!"

That day is past. . . .

This poem, like many others by Hughes, speaks with two voices—
the voice of the poet himself and the voice of the black Everyman
of the far-flung reaches of the black diaspora. There is also the suggestion of a third voice—the voice of the Communist revolutionary.
It is somewhat muted; but it is there, and the presence of this third
voice serves to explain the unusual publication history of this very

fine poem. The only time it was republished was as the title poem of the 1938 anthology *A New Song*. Even then, as Wagner clearly shows in his analysis of Hughes's poetry in *Les Poètes Nègres des États-Unis*, subtle changes were wrought in the poem's wording so that its second version reflected an "irreproachable religious orthodoxy." This was done by omitting any references to the possibility that the poet in particular and American Negroes in general had turned away from Jesus and Christianity as refuges in times of trouble and woe.

There is now considerable evidence at hand that Hughes, in his own statements and correspondence, sought to deemphasize his struggles during the 1930s with the black church and his involvement during that same time with international Communism. His comments in *The Big Sea* and *I Wonder as I Wander* are scarcely revelatory of any deep and abiding ideological commitment. Nor does his description of his encounter with evangelist Aimee Semple McPherson over the poem "Goodbye Christ" in his article "My Adventures as a Social Poet" (*Phylon*, 1947) give any hint of the extent of his disaffection with orthodox religion during this period. Fortunately, Faith Berry's *Good Morning Revolution*, an anthology of the poet's "uncollected writings of social protest" published in 1973, supplies considerable material which, properly evaluated, can help to set the record straight. In her introduction, she makes the point that, although "Hughes' most outspoken . . . poetry is from the 1930s," militant social protest is present in his poetry "as early as 1925." She also suggests, with considerable accuracy, that the poet's suppression of his Communist poetry does not reflect a cowardly attitude about a former ideological commitment but constitutes a very logical reaction to the almost neurotic polarization of American society into Communist and anti-Communist camps during the late 1940s and the 1950s. During that time, no publisher would have dared or been permitted to publish the writings of an author with proven Communist ties. It should be added in this context that any challenge to the accepted codes of religious orthodoxy could have had similarly devastating consequences on the perpetrator thereof, particularly if he were a black man attacking the black church. The reaction of Dr. Benjamin Mays to "Goodbye Christ," which will be noted below in greater detail, proves this point.

Good Morning Revolution furnishes clear evidence that by 1925 Hughes was a militant political radical. Indeed, this point is clearly stressed by Margaret Larkin in her article "A Poet for the People," published in *Opportunity* in March 1927. In her view, Hughes was, by virtue of poems like "Brass Spittoons," "Railroad Avenue," and

"Porter," already a proven "proletarian poet;" for all of these poems reflect a deep and abiding concern for the welfare and status of the working man. As the poet stated in *The Big Sea*, his wealthy sponsor, now identified as a Mrs. R. Osgood Mason, was fully unaware of how completely her young charge had turned from poetry that celebrated black exoticism and primitivism to poetry of militant social protest; therefore she could not understand how, in 1931, he could write a poem full of satire and ironic fury about the construction of the then fabulous Waldorf-Astoria or write in that same year:

> I live on a park bench.
> You, Park Avenue.
> Hell of a distance
> Between us two.
>
> I beg a dime for dinner—
> You got a butler and a maid.
> But I'm wakin' up!
> Say, ain't you afraid
>
> That I might, just maybe,
> In a year or two,
> Move on over
> To Park Avenue?

In "My Adventures as a Social Poet," Hughes stated that shortly after this poem was published, he "did not have a patron any more."

But there is more than militant social protest in "Pride," one of the poet's occasional pieces published in *Opportunity* in 1930; it smolders with the threat of revolutionary violence:

> Let all who will
> Eat quietly the bread of shame.
> I cannot,
> Without complaining loud and long,
> Tasting its bitterness in my throat,
> And feeling to my very soul
> Its wrong.
> For honest dreams
> Your spit is in my face,
> And so my fist is clenched—
> Today—
> To strike your face.

Significantly, none of the standard rhetoric of Communist propaganda appears in this poem, but its lines clearly reveal the poet's belief in the need for revolutionary change or, as he wrote in February 1931, a need to

> ... cut the world in two
> And see what worms are eating
> At the rind.

So there is every indication that, by 1930, the year he published *Not Without Laughter*, Langston Hughes had long been predisposed to support and endorse a program of radical social and economic change. His trip to Haiti and Cuba in 1930–31 and his return to an America engulfed in the shame of the Scottsboro trial were undoubtedly the catalysts that converted him into a poet of Communist propaganda.

Critical reactions to the poet's involvement in international Communism are mixed. Jean Wagner, whose study of Hughes includes the most extensive analysis of his Communist propaganda poetry to date, concludes that the poet's Communist poetry is "irredeemably false." Not only are these poems, in Wagner's view, innocent of "subversive import," but they reflect a "naivete and childishness" which negate serious political intent. Wagner supports his conclusion by citing Charles Glicksberg's opinion that, in general, all American Negroes are so "deeply rooted in the American tradition" that they yearn, not for Communism but for fulfillment of "the promises of democracy." Glicksberg's opinion, stated in an article on "Race and Revolution in Negro Literature," (*Forum*, Nov. 1947), undoubtedly reflected the general post-World War II belief that Communism had indeed been a "light that failed," not only for Hughes and Richard Wright but for all other Negro intellectuals and writers as well. Generally, this is the point of view of Wilson Record whose *The Negro and the Communist Party* (1951) has been termed the definitive study on the subject. Indeed, in a later article published in *Phylon* in 1956 ("Extremist Movements among American Negroes"), Record states that the Negro's disaffection with the Communist party stemmed from his inability to accept "the separate Negro state in the Black Belt proposal." According to Record, many Negro intellectuals, fearing the reimposition of social and economic segregation and separatism, abandoned the Communist cause for this reason. This interpretation is supported by James O. Young in his *Black Writers of the Thirties* (1973). In his view (p. 39):

Although . . . the young radicals often sympathized with such
Communist proposals as black-white labor solidarity and destruction of free-enterprise capitalism, they were never as far
left as the 'reds.' They remained independent of the Party and
were frequently critical of its policies.

Young's conclusion is that none of the Negro thinkers who leaned
toward the political left ever "condoned the idea of revolution."

But the opinions of Glicksberg and Record reflect after-the-fact
generalizations published during a period of near political hysteria
regarding Communism. Similarly, Young's comments attempt to
deemphasize the Negro's role in leftist revolutionism and drape him
in the robes of local patriotism. Persons nearer the scene of the
Negro's involvement in Communism in the 1930s can possibly provide more reliable evidence about the participation of Negro intellectuals in general and about Langston Hughes's involvement in
particular. According to Harold Cruse, for instance, the "leading
literary lights of the 1920's" all went into Communism in the 1930s
because they suffered from an "identity vacuum," caused by their
failure as a "black intelligentsia" to develop a unifying cultural philosophy. Upon analysis, this typically Crusian generalization apparently applies only to McKay and Hughes, both of whom became
involved with Communism, and not to Du Bois, Bontemps, Toomer, Johnson, or Cullen, all of whom did not. Given the context
of his comment, however, one gathers that accuracy was not Cruse's
concern here; rather, he wished to stress that he considered Communism a poor substitute for a unifying Negro cultural philosophy.
On the other hand, both Nick Aaron Ford and Sterling Brown, now
seasoned and retired professors of literature, were relatively young,
on-the-scene critics of the Negro literature of the 1930s, and their
comments are more specifically useful than Cruse's generalization.
Ford in his *Contemporary Negro Novels* (1936) gives approving
recognition of the trend of Negro novelists to lay aside "the pre-
tensions of pure artistry" and take up "the cudgel of propaganda."
Similarly, Sterling Brown, speaking before the National Negro
Congress in 1937, claimed that

the Negro artist who will be worth his salt must join with those
who are recording a world of injustice and exploitation—a
world that must be changed.

Earlier, George Schuyler in an article in *Opportunity* (June
1932) reviewing Roy Embree's *Brown America*, called for an end

to the "exploitation" of Negro labor and an end to "petite Negro bourgeois professional folk" who aid in such exploitation. What was needed, said Schuyler, were Negroes "who are well equipped leaders and organizers of the working class with proletarian instead of capitalistic psychologies." By 1936, Alain Locke in his annual review of Negro literature observes, with more than a tinge of regret (p. 7):

> our art is . . . turning prosaic, partisan, and propagandistic, but this time not in behalf of striving, strident racialism, but rather in a protestant and belligerent universalism of social analysis and protest. In a word, our art is going proletarian. . . .

And because proletarianism in art and literature bred a naturalism which was somewhat offensive to the refined sensibilities of Mr. Locke, he added that in this new breed of literature "all the slime and hidden secrets of the river [of racial experience] are shouldered up on the hard, gritty sandbars and relentlessly exposed to view."

There are other indices of the extent of Negro involvement in political radicalism and Communism during the 1930s. First, some of the more influential publishing media of the day carried reports on this as a matter of newsworthy comment. The *Chicago Defender*, for instance, headlined an editorial "Why We Can't Hate Reds" and praised "the zealousness with which [the Communist Party] guards the rights of the [Negro] Race." And in an editorial in *Crisis*, "Negro Editors on Communism" (April 1932, pp. 117-18), Carl Murphy of the *Afro-American* was quoted as saying, "The Communists are going our way, for which Allah be praised." William Kelley of the *Amsterdam News* had a comment of similar import:

> Since America's twelve million Negro population is so largely identified with the working class, the wonder is not that the Negro is beginning, at least, to think along Communistic lines, but that he did not embrace that doctrine en masse long ago.

In May of that same year, John Gillard, in a *Commonweal* article entitled "The Negro Challenges Communism" (May 25, 1932), observed:

> On the surface it would seem that Russian red and American black is a coming color scheme. Why not? The Negro has a grievance. Christians refuse to heed it. Communism listens

sympathetically. And when men are hungry and their children are fainting for bread, a promise seems better than a threat. Most of us who are not ourselves nursing the ills of poverty have a feeling of aloofness from the misery of our colored brother.

Another, albeit somewhat negative, index of Negro involvement in Communism is found in the impassioned response of those conservative Negro leaders who abhorred and feared that involvement. In 1933 *Opportunity* ran two articles of this category. The first by Asbury Smith sought to answer the question "What Can the Negro Expect from Communism?" (July 1933). Unfortunately, the question is never fully answered, but Smith does state the three reasons why, in his opinion, Negroes should not join the party. These are: (1) "Class Warfare" would not bring "economic justice"; (2) a dictatorship of the proletariat would result in a further and more intensive "restraint of democracy, censorship, and rule by fear and force"; and (3) the Negro en masse could not and would not abandon his religion and "share the Communist hatred of the worship of God." His conclusion clearly reflects the racial hostility hovering in the American atmosphere:

> If the Negroes accept Communism more rapidly than the whites, they will be oppressed with a cruelty and relentlessness unknown since Civil War Days.

Kelley Miller in his article "Should Black Turn Red?" (Nov. 1933) voiced a similar fear:

> not only would a communistic state in America put the Negro outside the pale, but the agitation for such a state on his part is fraught with grave peril to his race whose only hope for salvation lies in the fulfillment of the principles laid down in the Declaration of Independence and the Constitution of the United States.

In other words, Negro involvement in Communism and leftist political activity was a live and provocative issue in the 1930s. Admittedly, the rural masses of the agricultural South were never touched by the movement, but urban intellectuals, writers, and political polemicists were deeply involved. Langston Hughes was no exception. As Faith Berry's anthology *Good Morning Revolution* proves, the move to collaborate on matters of social protest with

Communists in the 1930s constituted no giant ideological step for the poet. Hughes's poetry of the mid-1920s reveals a strong predisposition for programs of radical social and political change. For somehow, despite his avid concern for jazz and blues and cabaret nightlife and his vaunted reputation as the somewhat feckless folk singer of the urban masses, Hughes, early in his publishing career, demonstrated an abiding concern for social, political, and economic justice for these Negro masses. Even as he sang of Africa, "So long/ So far away" and of "the low beating of the tom-toms," the seeds of political radicalism were being planted. They bore fruit when he returned from Haiti and Cuba in 1931 and discovered an America inflamed with the Scottsboro trial. His political sensitivities had already been ruffled by his temporary exclusion from Cuba by that country's immigration authorities. In his account of the incident in "My Adventures as a Social Poet" (*Phylon*, 1947), Hughes attributed the incident to the fact that he "had written poems about the exploitation of Cuba by the sugar barons." He also speculated that the "dictatorial Machado regime" might have objected to his translation of some of Nicolás Guillén's politically "radical" poetry, such as "Cane":

> White man
> Above the cane fields
> Earth
> Beneath the cane fields.
> Blood that flows from us.

But the imprisonment of nine young Negro boys, charged with raping two hoboing white prostitutes on a freight train near Scottsboro, Alabama, ignited within the poet all of the latent and smoldering fires of social, political, and racial protest. Typically, he wrote out his anger in poetry. The result was "Scottsboro," an occasional poem that appeared in *Opportunity* in December 1931, and has never again been reprinted, not even in the Communist-inspired *A New Song*.

8 BLACK BOYS IN A SOUTHERN JAIL.
WORLD, TURN PALE!

8 black boys and one white lie.
Is it much to die?

Is it much to die when immortal feet
March with you down Time's street,

When beyond steel bars sound the deathless drums
Like a mighty heart-beat as They come?

Who comes?

Christ,
Who fought alone.

John Brown.

That mad mob
That tore the Bastile down
Stone by stone.

Moses.

Jeanne d'Arc.

Dessalines.

Nat Turner.

Fighters for the free.

Lenin with the flag blood red.

(Not dead! Not dead!
None of those is dead.)

Gandhi.

Sandino.

Evangelista, too,
To walk with you—

8 BLACK BOYS IN A SOUTHERN JAIL.
WORLD, TURN PALE!

These lines reflect little evidence of the influence of Communist propaganda. Indeed, the poem's apparent objective is to identify the cause of the Scottsboro boys with those of the great martyrs of the world, living and dead; and the list is a distinguished honor roll, fully proving the passionate idealism of the poet's racial protest. Hughes's next publication on behalf of the Scottsboro boys, however, was fully in the Communist mold. *Scottsboro Limited*, four poems and a play, was written and presented in early 1932 in order to earn money for the International Labor Defense, the organization within the party designated to defend the Scottsboro boys. Not only does the short play depicting the arrest, trial, and imprisonment of the youths end with "a great red flag rising to the strains

of the *Internationale*," but throughout the short work there are lines
like the following:

> The voice of the red world
> Is our voice, too
> The voice of the red world is you!
>
> With all the workers,
> Black or white,
> We'll go forward
> Out of the night.

Alain Locke, who during the 1930s closely monitored Hughes's
literary career through his annual reports on Negro literature in
Opportunity, wrote the following evaluation of *Scottsboro Limited* in January 1933:

> Meanwhile, as the folk-school tradition deepens, Hughes, for-
> merly its chief exponent, turns more and more in the direction
> of social protest and propaganda, since *Scottsboro, Ltd.* repre-
> sents his latest moods. . . . The poet [in this work] is a militant
> and indignant proletarian reformer.

Locke's comments implicitly suggest that Hughes's gradual poetical
metamorphosis from folk poet to "indignant proletarian reformer"
was unfortunate. As has been indicated above, however, the line between folk poet and social reformer was a very thin line for a poet
like Langston Hughes. Moreover, in the spring of 1932, the poet
had visited the Scottsboro boys in their prison at Kilby, Alabama,
and recorded his reaction to that experience in an emotionally-
charged account ("Brown America in Jail: Kilby," *Opportunity*,
June 1932). Immediately following the prison visit, he wrote out
his anger about the gross injustice of Alabama law in a short piece
entitled "Christ in Alabama." This poem, with lines beginning
"Christ is a Nigger/Beaten and black" appeared in *Contempo*, a
University of North Carolina student publication just prior to
Hughes's lecture at the university in the same spring of 1932. The
unfortunate result, as recorded in "My Adventures as a Social
Poet," was that the poet's presence caused a near race riot. Shortly
afterwards, along with certain other American Negro writers and
actors, Hughes was on his way to Russia, ostensibly to make a movie
but actually in flight from a depression-ridden, racially volatile
America. So, by the time Alain Locke's comments appeared in *Opportunity* in January 1933, the poet was in Moscow and shiveringly

preparing himself to write a volume of short stories eventually entitled *The Ways of White Folks*. According to a note in Jean Wagner's *Les Poètes Négres des États-Unis*, Hughes, before his departure in July 1932, had declared his belief that Communism "was the only force leading an active fight against the poverty and wretchedness of Negroes." It is widely known that because he found Communism's regimentation of artists and writers too restrictive, the poet never became a card-carrying member of the party; but, as will be noted in greater detail below, he never disavowed his belief that during the depression years the American Negro had better friends in Moscow than in Macon County, Alabama.

Predictably, during his stay in Russia and following his return to America via Vladivostock and the Pacific, Hughes poured out Communist propaganda poetry. One poem, "Good Morning, Revolution," promises social upheaval and radical change with these lines:

> Listen, Revolution,
>   We're buddies, see—
>   Together,
>   We can take everything:
>   Factories, arsenals, houses, ships,
>   Railroads, forests, fields, orchards,
>   Bus lines, telegraphs, radios,
>   (Jesus! Raise hell with radios!)
>   Steel mills, coal mines, oil wells, gas,
>   All the tools of production,
>   (Great day in the morning!)
>   Everything—
>   And turn 'em over to the people who work.
>   Rule and run 'em for us people who work.

And there is even more fierce resolve in a poem entitled "Revolution" published in *New Masses* in February 1934:

> Great Mob that knows no fear—
> Come here!
> And raise your hand
> Against this man
> Of iron and steel and gold
> Who's bought and sold
> You—
> Each one—

For the last thousand years.
Come here,
Great mob that knows no fear,
And tear him limb from limb,
Split his golden throat
Ear to ear,
And end his time forever,
Now—
This year—
Great mob that knows no fear.

These lines literally crackle with the promise of revolutionary violence and confirm that the Langston Hughes of the mid-1930s was, in his outspoken social and political militancy, a far cry from the image of the "cool" poet projected in the 1951 poem, "Motto"—a poet who "never became a fanatical supporter of any one cause." These lines also contradict one of the conclusions in Arthur Davis's "Langston Hughes: Cool Poet" (*CLA Journal*, 1968), namely, that the poet "was never a fanatic and impassioned leftist." In the heat of his youth, like many other young poets, Hughes was deeply committed and in hot poetic pursuit of racial and economic justice. That his ardor for such causes "cooled" with the years was natural and inevitable. Certainly, Davis's assessment of Hughes as a somewhat detached and slightly amused observer of America's comedy of racial and social errors is fully accurate for the years immediately following World War II. But the poems and statements of the 1930s, which in so many instances were diligently suppressed by the poet, reveal a Langston Hughes who was an implacable and articulate advocate of revolutionary violence.

Hughes's 1953 statement before the congressional Committee on Government Operations stressed that his support of the political left during the 1930s was motivated by Communism's interest "in the problems of poverty, minorities, colonial peoples, and particularly of Negroes and Jim Crow." The record indicates that he was also convinced that the Negro's problems were in a large sense economic and that one way to help the Negro laborer was to have him link arms and causes with the white laborer, not only in America but throughout the world. By the mid-1930s, the poet had traveled enough to know that the "Black Seed" of the African diaspora had been "Driven before an alien wind" and left to exist "in soil/That's strange and thin." The rich progeny of Africa was to be found in the Caribbean, on the islands of the Atlantic and throughout the Americas; indeed, isolated pockets of "Black Seed" were scattered like "hybrid plants" throughout the world. And wherever blacks found themselves, they were economically destitute and politically oppressed. His poem, "The Same," published in the *Negro Worker* in 1932, defines the problem and suggests a Communist solution:

> It is the same everywhere for me:
> On the docks at Sierra Leone,
> In the cotton fields of Alabama,
> In the diamond mines of Kimberley
> On the coffee hills of Haiti,
> The banana lands of Central America,
> The streets of Harlem,
> And the cities of Morocco and Tripoli.
> Black:
> Exploited, beaten, and robbed,
> Shot and killed.
> Blood running into
>
>> DOLLARS
>> POUNDS
>> FRANCS
>> PESETAS
>> LIRE
>
> The force that kills,
> The power that robs,
> And the greed that does not care
> Better that my blood makes one with the blood
> Of all the struggling workers in the world
> Till every land is free of
>
>> DOLLAR ROBBERS
>> POUND ROBBERS
>> FRANC ROBBERS
>> PESETA ROBBERS
>> LIRE ROBBERS
>> LIFE ROBBERS—
>
> Until the Red Armies of the International Proletariat
> Their faces, black, white, olive, yellow, brown,
> Unite to raise the blood-red flag that
> Never will come down!

Interestingly enough, this poem not only presents a ringing affirmation of the value of a Communist solution for the bitter economic plight of the colored peoples of the world, but it presents the other

side of the coin of what came to be called "négritude," or an awareness of the worldwide cultural unity of the sons and daughters of
Africa. Here Hughes's emphasis is upon black economic exploitation and need; later Senghor, Césaire, and Damas stressed the cultural unity that helped black people endure and survive the pain of
that exploitation and need.

Langston Hughes's interest in Communism and its social and
economic panaceas culminated poetically with his publication of
A New Song, the small volume of poetry brought out by the International Worker's Order in 1938. It contains a somewhat changed
version of the original "New Song" published in 1933, as well as
other earlier occasional poems like "Park Bench," "Pride," and
"The Ballad of Lenin." In addition, there are new poems of Communist propaganda—"Chant for Tom Mooney," "Chant for May
Day," "Song of Spain," and "Union," a poem in which the poet
asks for "White and black" to "put their hands with mine/To
shake the pillars of those temples/Wherein false gods dwell/And
worn-out altars stand."

In general, literary critics of the 1930s responded only slightly
or not at all to Hughes's leftist and Communist propaganda poetry.
Certainly the muted critical response was nothing remotely com-
parable to the splendid furor that followed the poet's publication
of jazz and blues poems in the 1920s. Black critics of the day were
particularly silent and unresponsive. Of course, early in the decade
Du Bois had departed from the *Crisis* and therefore was not present
to provide critical leadership in his attack on the group of writers
whom he dismissed as spokesmen for "the debauched tenth." Brawley, a defender of the cause of the "talented tenth," continued to
publish his critical opinions, observations, and assessments, but his
efforts led him into troubled critical waters.

In 1934, for instance, in an essay "The Promise of Negro Literature" (*Journal of Negro History*), he advocated that Negro literature return to old verities and ancient truths: "The day of infla-
tion, of extravagance, of sensationalism is gone, and we must now
come back to earth and to a truer sense of values." This observation,
made in the midst of the greatest depression the world had ever
experienced, bespeaks a serious misreading of literary trends and
events. Predictably, Brawley's *Negro Genius* (1937) fully demonstrates that he was not au courant with literary events of the time.
He excoriates Hughes for the vulgarity of his jazz and blues poetry
of the previous decade but pointedly ignores any mention of the
leftist poetry which Hughes had been writing for several years. In
his review of *Negro Genius* (1937), Sterling Brown notes this fact

as one of the weaknesses of Brawley's treatment of Hughes ("Hughes's later poems of radical propaganda are neglected"), but Brown refused or thought it impolitic to speculate about the competence of his then senior Howard University colleague to evaluate "poems of radical propaganda." It may have been that to Brawley these were not poems at all, for many of the respected critics of the day stoutly maintained that propaganda was not literature and literature, hence, could never be mere propaganda. Brown does state in *Negro Poetry and Drama* (1937b), in his brief evaluation of the poetry of Hughes, that the poet's "most recent work is Communist propaganda" and that his "awakened interest in Communism has resulted in such poems as 'Goodbye Christ,' . . . 'The Ballad of Lenin,' . . . and 'The Ballad of Roosevelt.' " But possibly because of the pressures of time and space or the limitations of his critical method, he added no critical assessment of Hughes's poetry of Communist propaganda.

Similarly, Saunders Redding in his urbanely critical account of the poetry of Hughes in *To Make a Poet Black* (1939) considers his folk and racial protest poetry only and makes no mention of the poetry of Communist propaganda. This lack of critical comment tends to confirm the suspicion that the canons of critical taste that placed some constraints on a Benjamin Brawley also limited the critical range of many another literary expositor. Indeed, one is led to speculate that if the poets and novelists of the 1930s could have stopped their abhorrent practice of confusing literature with propaganda, then Brawley's prayerful request that "writers come back to earth and to a truer sense of values" would have been granted.

Fortunately, one Negro critic, Alain Locke, had both the critical temerity and esthetic insight to question the critical canon that propaganda was not and could never be literature. He did not reach this plateau of belief easily or quickly, however. In fact, during the 1920s when the issue of art versus propaganda was one of the lively topics of debate among Negro writers and intellectuals, Locke had defended the position that the only proper and fitting function of literature was to serve the ends of truth and beauty. Above all, he believed that the Negro's literature was never to be used to propagandize racial causes. Opposing him were Du Bois, Brawley, and a formidable array of racial leaders who believed that a wholesome literature devoted to the cause of racial uplift was the best propaganda for promoting racial integration. Locke's position was articulated in an article entitled "Art or Propaganda—Which?," published in *Harlem* (1928), a short-lived, one-issue periodical, edited by Wallace Thurman. Locke wrote, "After Beauty, let Truth come into the Renaissance picture." In his view, propaganda was merely a monotonous outpouring of the "Jeremiahs" who opposed "Truth and Beauty." In 1928, the "Jeremiahs" were Du Bois and those who joined him to lament the gross immorality of Negro art and literary expression not dedicated to the causes of integration and racial uplift.

With the beginning of the decade of the 1930s, Locke still held the view that literature should never be confused with propaganda. Writers who fell into propagandistic ways were chided by him in his annual reviews of Negro literature in *Opportunity*. In one issue he lamented that Hughes was no longer the folk poet that he had been but praised the novel *Not Without Laughter* because it palpitated "with the real spiritual essences of Negro life" and evoked "the folk temperament" as "truly and reverently" as his poetry had done earlier. But a lull in poetic creativity was to be expected, argued Locke, and he confidently predicted that Negro literature of the 1930s would be a "literature of criticism and interpretation" rather than a "literature·of creative expression." Or, as the critic somewhat flamboyantly expressed the matter, "the buoyant Renaissance" was about to be followed by a reenforcing "sober Reformation." By the middle of the decade, in an annual review provocatively entitled "The Eleventh Hour of Nordicism," (*Opportunity*, Jan. 1935), Locke again lamented that "the poetic strain" in Negro literature "has dwindled in quantity and quality" and that the "occasional poems of Cullen and Hughes are below the level of their earlier work." But by this time he had developed a critical theory to explain the temporary demise of the poetic arts. He wrote: "Evidently, it is not the hour for poetry, nor should it be—this near noon of a prosaic, trying day." For, he continued

> Poets, like birds, sing at dawn and dusk; they are hushed by the heat of propaganda and the din of work and battle and become vocal only before and after as the heralds or the caroling serenaders.

Fortified with this somewhat archaic and romantic notion of the poetical function, Locke then proceeded to condemn the poetry section of Nancy Cunard's *Negro Anthology* (1934), to which Hughes had contributed several Communist propaganda pieces, as nothing more than "hot rhetoric and clanging emotion." Similarly, Hughes's volume of short stories, *The Ways of White Folks*, Locke described as being "avowedly propagandistic and motivated by a radical social philosophy."

However, a change in his critical attitude is seen in his review, "Jingo, Counter-Jingo and Us" (*Opportunity*, Jan. 1938). This essay, largely written in reaction to Benjamin Stolberg's article "The Minority Jingo" (*Nation*, Oct. 23, 1937) starts with a discussion of the levels of jingoism in matters literary. In Locke's view, there was not only a "minority jingo," so clearly demonstrated in Brawley's *Negro Builders and Heroes* (1934) with its "artistically indigestible minority chauvinism" and "Pollyanna sentimentalism," but there were other kinds of jingoism—a majority jingo (to which a minority jingo always reacted), a proletarian jingo, a bourgeois jingo, a capitalist jingo, as well as jingos of "the credal and racial varieties." As the article proceeds, it becomes clear that in Locke's view a jingo was no more than a propagandistic stance or point of view held by a given author. In the end, Locke argues himself into the conclusion that "good art" can develop from "sound and honest propaganda," but "dishonest propaganda" would always result in bad art or bad literature. Two other interesting conclusions are that the "Negro cause in literature" has been plagued by "bad art and the blight of false jingo" and that the "New Negro movement" of the previous decade was "choked in shallow cultural soil by the cheap weeds of group flattery, vainglory and escapist emotionalism." Thus in this review of the Negro literature of 1937, Alain Locke took two giant steps in critical belief: he recognized that propaganda can have a place in literature or art, and he finally was able to place the "fervent creativity" of the Harlem Renaissance in more balanced critical perspective. Undoubtedly, these changes in his critical outlook enabled Locke to be more understanding of Langston Hughes's Communist and racial propaganda poetry and prepared him to greet the rising new genius of Richard Wright with greater critical sympathy.

So using the critical criteria that honest propaganda can produce good literature and bad propaganda can result in bad literature, Locke approached Hughes's *A New Song*. He found the little volume a far cry, qualitatively speaking, from what Hughes had produced earlier. The poet had used, said Locke, "a twangy lyre" in writing these poems of racial protest and Communist propaganda. Even armed with his more enlightened critical credo about propagandistic literature, Locke found nothing poetically inspiring in lines exhorting workers of "The black / And White World" to arise, unite, and revolt. Nor did he consider poems like "Chant for May Day," with its rather ambitious orchestration for group recitation, of a very high poetic order. But the critic did make a critical exception of two poems in the slender volume; these were the

"Ballad of Ozzie Powell" and "The Song of Spain." This last poem, although never included in any later collections of Hughes's poetry, had a special appeal to Locke and others who were sensitized to the political and social events surrounding the Spanish Civil War. Evidently, some of the emotional power of this poem stems from the fact that it contains Hughes's initial reaction to the war and to the death in that war of fellow poet Federico Garcia Lorca.

Few of the many later critical commentaries on Hughes's poetry contain specific observations about his leftist or Communist propaganda poetry. Undoubtedly, this trend was attributable to the temper of the times. With the cold war, there was an inevitable cooling of interest in any kind of literature that was sympathetic with Communism or with the Soviet Union. This is even true of critical works with a Third World emphasis, such as *The Militant Black Writer* (1969) by Mercer Cook and Stephen Henderson. In this very provocative study of African literary protest and the black cultural and political revolution of the 1960s, stress is placed—and rightly so—on the role played by Langston Hughes in stimulating African literary protest and promoting the revolution of black consciousness in black America. In such a context, any discussion of the poet's earlier involvement with political radicalism would, in one sense, appear to be irrelevant. For what could the integrationist revolutionism of pre-World War II Communism have to do with the revolution for black separatism of the 1960s? The answer lies in ascertaining the cause and motivation for one's involvement in the promotion of a revolutionary cause. It is evident from the thematic thrust of his Communist propaganda poetry that Hughes's principal objective in the 1930s was to improve the lot of black people, not only in America but throughout the world. Viewed in retrospect, the enabling political machinery that he chose to use—International Communism—was of questionable value; but many during that time who were desperate for change saw this as the one viable means to achieve the kind of economic and social revolution needed to lift black people out of the abyss of colonial oppression. For this reason, it may be argued that the Hughes of the 1930s was a singularly dedicated militant black writer whose assault on American race prejudice was sustained, vigorous, and unrelenting.

Unfortunately, the one critic of Hughes's poetry who has discussed his leftist poetry in some detail does not agree with this conclusion. To Jean Wagner in his *Les Poètes Négres des États-Unis*, the Communist propaganda poetry of Langston Hughes was more rhetorical than ideological—more a participatory rite in a popular trend than a deep commitment to a revolutionary cause. Reflected in this judgment is the view shared by some that generally Hughes's commitment to causes was never deep and abiding but controlled by surface trends and popular vogues. François Dôdat, in his *Langston Hughes* (1964, p. 52), articulates this opinion as follows:

> This poet is not a thinker, but nobody would dream of reproaching him for it, because, on the contrary, he possesses an extraordinary faculty for defining the confused sensations that constitute the collective conscience of simple minds.

This observation damns the poet with a faint praise that, in view of Wagner's predilection for poets who are prophets and thinkers, would probably raise that critic's esteem for Hughes not one iota. In fact, behind Wagner's conclusion that "in all this Communist propaganda one senses something *irredeemably false*" [italics mine] is the unqualified assumption that all of Hughes's poetry in this vein was mere rhetorical pose. One speculates whether Wagner makes this inference primarily because the poet made no on-the-record, life-and-death commitment to Communism. If he had, Wagner seems to ask, how could Hughes have then made his well-known comment about his inability to give up jazz in order to promote world revolution. If the poet had been firmly and irrevocably committed, he would not only have joined the party and become an official, card-carrying member, but he would have "gone to school" in the literature, philosophy, and political methodology of international Communism. In other words, one is led to infer that to Wagner a commitment to party was like a commitment to religion —a commitment that prohibited casual levity or occasional deviation from either the creed or the discipline. Obviously, if a man has made no such commitment, no one can take seriously his protestations for that cause or creed. Therefore, Wagner observes (p. 436):

> It is a trifling startling to think that the U.S. Senate should have called a committee of investigation into session to examine these works [Hughes's Communist propaganda writings] whose naïvete and childishness far outweigh their subversive import.

Not only does this statement indicate that Wagner is himself very "naive" about the average Senate committee's reputation for "investigative efficiency," but it also implies certain defects in his own critical method. In the first place, his analysis of Hughes's Communist propaganda poetry does not lead to, nor support, his conclu-

sion that the poems are naive and childish. In his discussion of the
literature, Wagner stresses the poet's emphasis on the need of a true
union of black and white labor and on how the "solidarity of the
world proletariat" would, in Hughes's view, end the ubiquitous
exploitation of black labor. The critic also discusses the principal
message of *Scottsboro Limited*—that with the help of Communists
the Scottsboro boys will ultimately be freed—but there is no hint in
his comments that what the poet wrote on behalf of the Scottsboro
boys was either naive or childish. In the second place, the words
"naivete and childishness" have little or no meaning in the lexicon
of literary criticism. Not only do they suggest a kind of hyperbo-
lism or overstatement that good critics tend to avoid, but it is difficult to conclude what Wagner means by his use of these terms. Is
his reference to the political simplicity of these poems? Or are the
poet's pleas for violent revolution the utterances of a political un-
sophisticate who has no comprehension of the real sources of economic and political power? Unfortunately, there is nothing in
Wagner's critical text to suggest an answer. In the third place, it
appears that the critical method employed here is defective simply
because Wagner permits a seemingly authoritative secondary
source (Charles Glicksberg's "Race and Revolution in Negro Literature," 1947) to dictate his critical conclusion, even though there
is nothing in his own analysis that leads to or supports such a conclusion. Finally, Wagner's critical method is suspect here because,
by his own admission, his conclusion is based on inadequate evidence. In a footnote to his critical discussion (p. 436), the critic
states:

> The poems just cited are probably not the only poems written
> by Hughes in this vein, and it should be possible to find others
> in various periodicals. But as it was our intention to throw light
> on one facet of the poet's work, not to take issue with the opin-
> ions held by the man, we did not believe any useful purpose
> could have been served by continuing our researches in this
> direction.

This oddly illogical statement speaks for itself.

Over and beyond deficiencies in critical method, Wagner's discussion of Hughes's poetry of Communist propaganda justifies two
other general observations about the value of his criticism. First, in
taking Hughes's measure as a dedicated Communist revolutionary,
Wagner is obviously using a Gallic yardstick. He wants tangible
and incontrovertible evidence of some group alignment and involve-

ment. Like the chroniclers of old who demanded of knights-errant proof of their "errantry," Wagner apparently demands specific proof over and beyond any yielded by the words of a poem or a trip to Russia or a journey to the scene of the Spanish Civil War. Using the Gallic yardstick of formal and legalistic participation, Wagner seems to be saying that adherence to party regulation and compliance with party discipline, preferably at some personal sacrifice, are the only truly valid forms of proof of one's Communist involvement. If evidence of such activity is lacking, then one's expressions and actions on behalf of the party become "irredeemably false" expressions and actions. In other words, Langston Hughes enjoyed far too much individual flexibility, American-style, to meet Wagner's somewhat rigid and essentially Gallic (or European) criterion for true partisan commitment. Thus, what appears to be Wagner's somewhat patronizing devaluation of Hughes's Communist commitment undoubtedly reflects his own background and general orientation about the nature of political partisanship.

Nor does this French critic seem to have the background and general orientation which enable him to empathize fully with the trauma experienced by the victims of American racism. In justifying his involvement with Communism, Langston Hughes explained (and Wagner has a note acknowledging such an explanation) that Communism's efforts to alleviate "the poverty and wretchedness of Negroes" was the source of its appeal to him. And he made it clear in his poetry, in his plays, and in his short essays that the dilemma of the Scottsboro boys, sitting on death row in Kilby Prison in Alabama, was not only an affront to Christians everywhere but proof positive that American racial justice was a mockery and a delusion. For some reason, on this matter Wagner the critic never fully heard and understood Hughes the poet. Possibly, cultural and racial differences were too great. Possibly, the critic had not read enough about what the poet said about Scottsboro. Maybe he had not read "Brown America in Jail: Kilby" (*Opportunity*, June 1932), the short statement giving the poet's impressions of his visit to "the Negro wing" of a "Human zoo" where "Like monkeys in tiered cages, hundreds of Negroes" were "barred away from life." Possibly, Wagner had not read the poet's account of his sensations upon entering "the solid steel door" of the death house of Kilby's Negro wing:

> Dark faces peering from behind bars, like animals when the keeper comes. All Negro faces, men and young men in this death house at Kilby. Among them the eight Scottsboro boys.

> . . . Eight brown boys condemned to death. No proven crime.
> Farce of a trial. Lies. Laughter. Mob. Music. Eight poor nig-
> gers make a country holiday.

Hughes also presented in a speech before the American Writers'
Congress in 1939 some of the problems that he had encountered as
a Negro author in a segregated society, and what he wrote should
have built bridges of understanding with literary critics who, like
Wagner, were far removed from the American literary scene. One
particularly effective point in his address was that the publishing
business viewed the Negro as an exotic and therefore accepted from
the Negro author only exotic material; as Hughes put it, "When we
cease to be exotic, we do not sell well." Moreover, Hughes emphasized that in America the Negro author was denied "the common
courtesies of decent travel" and routinely excluded from "jobs as
professional writers, editorial assistants, and publisher's readers." So
to be a Negro writer in the America of the 1930s was an economically hazardous and, at times, emotionally unfulfilling experience.
For, as the poet had pointed out in his first speech before the American Writers' Congress in 1935, the tasks confronting the Negro
writer were heavy and arduous. First, he had to seek "to unite blacks
and whites" in America, "not on the nebulous basis of an interracial
meeting or on the shifting sands of religious brotherhood, but on
the *solid* ground of the daily working-class struggle to wipe out,
now and forever, all the old inequalities of the past." In addition,
Hughes called upon the Negro writer to expose "the lovely grin-
ning face of Philanthropy" which supports and sustains institutional
racism, and expose as well the "sick-sweet smile of organized religion which lies about what it does not know and about what it does
know." If these responsibilities were not enough for the already
over-burdened Negro author, the poet also charged him to

> Expose also, the false leadership that besets the Negro people—
> bought and paid for leadership, owned by capital, afraid to
> open its mouth except in the old conciliatory way so advan-
> tageous to the exploiters. . . . And the Contentment Tradition
> of the O-lovely-Negroes school of American fiction, which
> makes an ignorant black face and a Carolina head filled with
> superstition, appear more desirable than a crown of gold. . . .
> And expose war. And the old My-Country-Tis-of-Thee lie.

In other words, critics who, like Wagner, have attempted to
evaluate the poetic career of Langston Hughes from afar, as it were,

have long had access to materials which define that writer's philosophy of authorship and describe the social, moral, and political climate in which he had to function as an author. How these materials are employed by a given critic are, of course, determined by that critic's own critical philosophy. The point of emphasis here is that Hughes's leftist poetry of the 1930s was not written in a cultural, political, or emotional vacuum; and, as Wagner's fellow countryman Michel Taine once indicated, a literary work can not be fully assessed without some knowledge of the man who wrote it, the milieu that shaped and molded the writer's experience, and the moment that sparked his creativity.

That Wagner failed at times to develop such a recommended well-rounded view of Hughes is indicated by his treatment of the "Goodbye, Christ" episode in the poet's career. In 1932, just prior to, or immediately upon, his departure for Russia, the poet had written a poem bearing this title. In essence, it was a frank and direct attack on the Christian church and on organized religion in the United States and provoked such a controversy among both whites and blacks that it was never reprinted after its publication in *The Negro Worker* in November 1932. Indeed, so bitter and prolonged was the reaction from both the press and the pulpit that the poet felt compelled to issue an explanation of the poem's meaning in 1941, almost ten years after its publication. His short statement "Concerning 'Goodbye, Christ' " has to be considered if one is to read and interpret the poem in the light of the author's intended meaning. Following are some of the lines that provoked a bitter reaction on all levels of the "Establishment":

> Listen, Christ,
> You did alright in your day, I reckon—
> But that day's gone now.
> They ghosted you up a swell story, too
> Called it Bible—
> But it's dead now.
> The popes and the preachers've
> Made too much money from it.
> They've sold you to too many
>
> Kings, generals, robbers, and killers. . . .
>
> Goodbye,
> Christ Jesus Lord God Jehova
> Beat it on away from here now.
> Make way for a new guy with no religion at all—

> A real guy named
> Marx Communist Lenin Peasant Stalin Worker ME. . . .
>
> Go ahead on now . . .
> And please take Saint Gandhi with you when you go,
> And Saint Pope Pius,
> And Saint Aimee McPherson
> And big black Saint Becton
> Of the Consecrated Dime. . . .

Inevitably, this abrasively radical poem raised howls of indignation and rage from religionists everywhere and from many of the so-called guardians of the Establishment. An enraged Aimee Semple McPherson, popular evangelist of the Temple of the Four Square Gospel in Los Angeles, preached from her sanctified pulpit that Langston Hughes was "a red devil in a black skin." There is no record of a response from "big black Saint Becton," Harlem's popular and successful evangelist; but Dr. Benjamin Mays, serving as a spokesman for the black church, wrote in his *The Negro's God as Reflected in his Literature* (1938, p. 239)

> The case of Langston Hughes is clear. The absolute repudiation of Christ, God, and religion, and the reliance upon Marx, Lenin, and Stalin is the extreme left to which the negation of God . . . may lead.

He added that Hughes's case seemed to be typical of the "wave of cynicism, defeat and frustration in the writings of young Negroes where God is discussed."

In his short statement explaining the genesis and meaning of the poem, Hughes made essentially three points. First, he said that he found American-style racial segregation and its violent consequences "unbelievable in a Christian country." In 1931 he had made his first tour of the American South and was appalled by all that he saw and experienced; and it seemed to him that America itself, through its "apparent actions toward my people" was by its action as a nation officially saying "goodbye" to Christ and His principles of toleration, love, and spiritual friendship. Hughes's second point was that the "I" in the poem is not the poet himself but a persona compounded of "the newly liberated peasant of the state collectives" in Russia and "those American Negro workers of the depression period who believed in the Soviet dream." In other words, the "I" of the poem was designed to be a composite of white Communist laborer and black Communist laborer. In his explanation, the poet added that quite frequently, as in his blues poetry, he was not the "I" in his poems. One critic, Donald Gibson, explains this Hughesian practice as follows (p. 78):

> Hughes assumes a multitude of personae. At one time he is the spirit of the race who represents the Negro or Blackman, then he is a shoeshine boy, a black mother . . . a black man without a job or money, a prostitute, a ghetto tenant. Sometimes he is a consciousness where role is incapable of determination. And sometimes he speaks . . . as the poet.

Hughes's third point was that "Goodbye, Christ" was the product of the poet's "radical" twenties; and, since that time, he had moved to a new level of belief which asserted "that no system of ethics, religion, morals, or government is of permanent value which does not first start with and change the human heart."

In his comments on "Goodbye, Christ" Wagner appears to ignore Hughes's statement of explanation, although he admits to having received a copy of that statement (p. 438). Instead, he states his belief that the poem resulted from "a personal religious crisis" similar to the crisis which the poet had experienced at the age of thirteen in Lawrence, Kansas, and later described in *The Big Sea* (pp. 18-21). Wagner then equates (p. 439) Hughes's "spiritual frustration," evidenced in these crises, with that experienced by

> many intellectuals in the "talented tenth" who, resolutely determined on total emancipation, turned their backs both on the white man's Christianity, since they saw it as one of the last vestiges of enslavement that had survived the abolition of slavery, and the formalist religion of the traditional Negro churches, whose faded, simple-minded rituals did little to disguise the absence of a strong spirituality. . . .

In other words, Wagner's critical discussion of the poem drifts off the subject of the poem into a generalization of dubious relevancy and questionable validity. Certainly, he completely ignores Hughes's statement for the rationale of the poem. His conclusion about "Goodbye, Christ" is even more surprisingly illogical for, once again, the statements that precede the concluding comment have no direct and discernible cause-and-effect relationship with such a conclusion (p. 440):

> But in Hughes' case these rebellious gestures [against the church and organized religion] proved quite transitory. For

these were gestures only, and not those crises of conscience that seize upon certain delicate souls and shake them to their very depths. McKay, Toomer, and Cullen did not hesitate occasionally to estrange their fellows in order to follow the paths of the spirit. But Hughes was not of that dimension. . . .

Not only is the comparison of Hughes with his fellow black poets unsupported and therefore both irresponsible and irrelevant (and even possibly "full odious"), but the reasons for summarily reducing "two religious crises" to the level of merely "transitory rebellious gestures" are never given. One suspects that Wagner has to cope throughout his Hughes study with a worrying hypothesis, namely, that Hughes was never a poet in the grand manner but only a facile versifier—one who lived only on the surface of events and hence could never truly suffer a deep emotional crisis. A critic with his neck in the noose of such a hypothesis has to select his evidence very carefully, lest the noose grow uncomfortably tight. For this reason, Wagner finds Hughes's explanatory statement about "Goodbye, Christ" unusable, simply because it did not lead to his predetermined conclusion. This critical observation is supported by a note which Wagner appends to his comments (p. 440, n. 180):

> He [Hughes] was fully justified . . . in noting the all too blatant divergency between the doctrine and the practices of his adversaries. But if he had not remained at the surface of these problems, how could he persistently have avoided proceeding to the sounding of his own conscience? All things considered, religious problems are reduced to social problems in his eyes, while the richness and the complexities of the inner life seem to have been a closed book for him.

This note leads to Wagner's oft reiterated conclusion that Hughes did not have the inner dimensions which would have made him capable of a deep and abiding spiritual or emotional commitment. Such a conclusion, in the light of the poet's radical poetry of the 1930s, is quite untenable. During those years, the poet was committed as always to the cause of alleviating the economic and social distress of Negro people and fully convinced that Communism provided a feasible approach to attaining that objective.

In the 1953 statement which he read to the Senate subcommittee investigating his Communist involvement, Hughes said that his faith in Communism as an efficacious means of eradicating racial prejudice and economic inequality effectively dissipated with the signing of the Soviet-German nonaggression pact in 1939. The record indicates that this was true not only of Hughes but of many of his contemporaries who, at this point, became disenchanted with the *réalpolitik* of Communism. But further analysis of his poetry in the 1940s and 1950s will reveal that although he changed his mind about Communism, his commitment to the cause of Negro rights and freedom remained unchanged.

References

Berry, Faith
  1973. (editor) *Good Morning Revolution.* New York: Lawrence Hill.
Brawley, Benjamin
  1934. "The Promise of Negro Literature," *Journal of Negro History* 19:53–59.
  1937. *The Negro Genius.* New York: Dodd, Mead.
Brown, Sterling A.
  1937. "Review of *The Negro Genius,*" *Opportunity* Sept., pp. 280–81.
  1937b. *Negro Poetry and Drama.* Washington: Associates in Negro Folk Education.
Calverton, V. F.
  1940. "The Negro and American Culture," *Saturday Review of Literature* Sept., pp. 3–4.
Cruse, Harold
  1967. *The Crisis of the Negro Intellectual.* New York: Morrow.
Davis, Arthur
  1968. "Langston Hughes: Cool Poet," *CLA Journal* 40:280–96.
Dickinson, Donald C.
  1967. *A Bio-Bibliography of Langston Hughes, 1902-1967.* Hamden, Conn.: Shoe String.
Dôdat, François
  1964. *Langston Hughes.* Paris: Édition Seghers.
Ford, Nick Aaron
  1936. *The Contemporary Negro Novel: A Study in Race Relations.* Boston: Meador.
Gibson, Donald
  1971. "The Good Black Poet and the Good Gray Poet." In *Langston Hughes: Black Genius,* edited by Therman O'Daniel, pp. 65–80. New York: Morrow.
Gillard, John
  1932. "The Negro Challenges Communism," *Commonweal* May 25, p. 97.
Henderson, Stephen, and Mercer Cook
  1969. *The Militant Black Writer.* Madison: Univ. of Wisconsin Pr.

Hughes, Langston
1932. "Brown America in Jail: Kilby," *Opportunity* June, p. 174.
1935. *To Negro Writers.* A speech given in New York at the First American Writers' Congress. April.
1939. *Democracy and Me.* A speech given in New York at the Third American Writers' Congress. June.
1947. "My Adventures as a Social Poet," *Phylon* Fall, pp. 205–12.

Larkin, Margaret
1927. "A Poet for the People," *Opportunity* March, pp. 84–85.

Locke, Alain
1928. "Art or Propaganda—Which?" *Harlem* Nov., pp. 19–23.
1933. "Black Truth and Black Beauty," *Opportunity* Jan., pp. 14–18.
1935. "The Eleventh Hour of Nordicism," *Opportunity* Jan., pp. 4–10; part 2, pp. 46–48, 59.
1936. "Deep River, Deeper Sea," *Opportunity* Jan., pp. 6–10; part 2, pp. 42–43, 61.
1938. "Jingo, Counter-Jingo and Us," *Opportunity* Jan., pp. 7–11, 27; part 2, pp. 39–42.

Mays, Benjamin
1938. *The Negro's God as Reflected in his Literature.* Boston: Grimes and Chapman.

Miller, Kelley
1933. "Should Black Turn Red?" *Opportunity* Nov., pp. 328–32, 350.

O'Daniel, Therman
1971. (editor) *Langston Hughes: Black Genius.* New York: Morrow.

Redding, Saunders
1939. *To Make a Poet Black.* Chapel Hill: Univ. of North Carolina Pr.

Schuyler, George
1932. "Review of Edwin Embree's *Brown America*," *Opportunity* June, pp. 175–76.

Smith, Asbury
1933. "What Can the Negro Expect from Communism?" *Opportunity* July, pp. 211–12.

Wagner, Jean
1962. *Les Poètes Négres des États-Unis.* Paris: Librairie Ista.

Young, James O.
1973. *Black Writers of the Thirties.* Baton Rouge: Louisiana State Univ. Pr., p. 39.

CHAPTER 4

"Here
on the Edge of Hell"

Here on the edge of Hell
Stands Harlem. . . .

With the beginning of the 1940s, Langston Hughes returned to Harlem after a decade of international travel and involvement with worldwide politics, war, and assorted controversial causes. Some of the excitement and movement of the 1930s he later attempted to recapture in *I Wonder as I Wander* (1956), a carefully edited account of names, places, and events which he had seen and encountered during his world-circling search for meccas of promise which might relieve the world of political oppression and economic exploitation. In a sense, events conspired to force his return. Following the conclusion of the Spanish Civil War and the triumph of rightist forces in that war, it quickly became evident that what had happened on the Iberian peninsula was only a brief and bloody rehearsal for a holocaust of universal dimensions.

Inevitably, Hughes, a man deeply sensitized to new movements and events, reflected his reaction to World War II in his writings. The most beneficial result was the development of that urbanized version of the Negro Everyman of mid-century America, Jess B. Semple. Starting as a weekly series in the *Chicago Defender* and other newspapers, Hughes's anecdotes about the experiences and reflections of a Negro defense factory worker eventually expanded into five volumes of excellent comic fiction. In these stories, the poet demonstrated that one of his qualities as a writer was his ability to produce, through disciplined comic detachment and controlled dramatic objectivity, a composite and fully representative persona whose lively wit and common sense have endeared him to readers all over the world. As one views Hughes's writing career in retrospect, it appears that with Negro enclaves in America's cities hardening into crime-ridden, poverty-stricken ghettos, the poet found it ever more expedient and self-protective to don the mask of comic detachment which had worked so well in the production of the Simple stories. It was the only way for him to stay alive as a black creative writer. In this sense, the 1940s represent a sort of transition period between the impassioned radicalism of the 1930s and what Arthur Davis (*CLA Journal*, 1968) calls the "coolly ambivalent vision" and objective detachment of the 1950s and 1960s. If such a speculation be true, then the enormous success of the Simple stories was the main catalyst for this important change in authorial attitude.

The war also affected Hughes's writing career in other respects. The climate of the times with its emphasis on the euphoria of patriotic dedication forced him to return to an earlier theme—the promises inherent in the American dream. In the 1920s he had written of America's promise to give "the darker brother" a seat of equality at the banquet table of American rights and opportunities. Now, with emphasis on America's splendid legacy of freedom, Hughes again addressed his poetic attention to this subject with his *Freedom's Plow* (1943). First published in *Opportunity* (April 1943), the poem "*Freedom's Plow*" was written as a declamation piece for Paul Muni and featured on one of the radio programs of the Vocational Opportunity Program in March 1943. As Wagner indicates in his critical study of the poet in *Les Poètes Négres des États-Unis* (1962), Hughes successfully shows that the aspirations for freedom of Negro leaders like Frederick Douglass fully complemented those expressed by Jefferson and Lincoln. First there were the dreams of the freedom-searching individuals who had founded America; then, in Wagner's words, "From the pooling of these individual dreams ... there rose up the great communal dream called America." The French critic also effectively links the tone and spirit of "Freedom's Plow" to Whitman's poetry on America's democratic promise. Indeed, it is his opinion that, of all of Hughes's poetry, this poem is "the most Whitman-like," particularly in its emphasis on America as a dream held in common in the hearts of all the people. This point is also stressed by Donald Gibson in his article, "The Good Black Poet and the Good Gray Poet," (*Modern Black Poets*, 1973, pp. 43-56). In this critic's view, both Whitman and Hughes believed in democracy "because of its promise to do away with social distinctions." Both poets, says Gibson, were "democrats to the bone" believing in America's promise and America's dream. Or, as "the good black poet" wrote in "Freedom's Plow":

> A long time ago,
> An enslaved people heading toward freedom
> Made up a song:
>> *Keep Your Hand On the Plow! Hold On!*
> That plow plowed a new furrow

Across the field of history.
Into that furrow the freedom seed was dropped.
From that seed a tree grew, is growing, will ever grow.
That tree is for everybody,
For all America, for all the world.

It should be noted here that Gibson, before ending his very effective
comparison of the two American poets, does remark on "the good
gray poet's personal repugnance toward black people"—a fact nowhere apparent in *Leaves of Grass* and doubtless fully unknown to
"the good black poet." For Hughes had great admiration for "Old
Walt" who, in his words,

Went finding and seeking,
Finding less than sought
Seeking more than found,
Every detail minding
Of the seeking or the finding.

Wagner also sees evidence in "Freedom's Plow" of Hughes's
emphasis on America as a land in which the social, political, and
personal ambitions of all men would be fulfilled in a fair and equita-
ble society with abundant opportunities for all. In this sense, this
long wartime poem extolling America's promise and potential re-
iterates a theme that was present in Hughes's poetry from the beginning. In his first volume of poetry in 1926, he described himself
as "The Dream-Keeper"—one whose major poetic responsibility
was to preserve the dreams of others by wrapping "them/In a blue
cloud-cloth/Away from the too rough fingers/Of the world." And
in his short collection entitled *The Dream-Keeper*, published primarily for young readers in 1932, he wrote of the importance of
"Dreams":

Hold fast to dreams
For if dreams die
Life is a broken-winged bird
That cannot fly.

In the Hughesian context, dreams are in reality promises ("America is a dream/The poet says it was promises")—the promises of a
nation to its citizens, the promises of a man to himself. Any nation
or society courts spiritual and moral disaster if these promises are
not kept or when, for some reason, fulfillment is "deferred." For
instance, on Memphis's "Beale Street"

> The dream is vague
> And all confused
> With dice and women
> And jazz and booze. . . .
>
> The loss
> Of the dream
> Leaves nothing
> The same.

But Wagner argues—and quite rightly so—that Hughes, despite some moments of wavering faith and occasional embitterment, believed firmly what he wrote in the concluding lines of his poem "Oppression":

> Now dreams
> Are not available
> To the dreamers
> Nor songs to the singers. . . .
>
> But the dream
> Will come back
> And the song
> Break
> Its jail.

The poet believed that America could recover its dreams and find the spiritual and emotional renewal which was once its promise for all of its citizens. This is best expressed in "Let America Be America Again," a long patriotic poem with proletarian overtones first published in 1938 in *A New Song*:

> Let America be the dream the dreamers dreamed—
> Let it be that great strong land of love
> Where never kings connive nor tyrants scheme
> That any man be crushed by one above. . . .
>
> Oh yes,
> I say it plain
> America never was America to me
> And yet I swear this oath—
> America will be!

But even as the poet sought to confirm America as a land of promise and praised her strength as she prepared to do battle with the forces of fascism, Hughes retained, as mentioned earlier, what Arthur Davis has called his "ambivalent vision"—his ability to see both sides of a situation. As a counter to the patriotic zeal of the poems extolling the American dream, he wrote as follows in "Southern Negro Speaks," a poem published in *Opportunity* in October 1941:

> I reckon they must have
> Forgotten about me
> When I hear them say they gonna
> Save Democracy.
> Funny thing about white folks
> Wanting to go and fight
> Way over in Europe
> For freedom and light
> When right here in Alabama—
> Lord have mercy on me!
> They declare I'm a Fifth Columnist
> If I say the word, Free.
> Jim Crow all around me.
> Don't have the right to vote.
> Let's leave our neighbor's eye alone
> And look at our own mote—
> Cause I sure don't understand
> What the meaning can be
> When folks talk about freedom
> And Jim Crow me?

As a skilled and gifted dramatic monologuist, Hughes was able to examine all of the nuances of the American experience and speak with many voices. But, though he "never stopped needling America," to use Arthur Davis's phrase, the poet steadfastly retained the idealism expressed in these lines from his Haitian opera *Troubled Island* (1936):

> I dream a world where all
> Will know sweet freedom's way,
> Where greed no longer saps the soul
> Nor avarice blights our day.
>
> A world I dream where black or white
> Whatever race you be,
> Will share the bounties of the earth
> And every man is free....

There is no doubt that the Harlem of the 1940s severely tested the validity of the poet's dream and the idealism that nurtured the dream. For the economic depression of the 1930s had robbed Harlem of the bright effulgence it had enjoyed during the twenties. Not only had all of its promises wilted on the vine of compromise and racist politics, but its inhabitants had become uncertain and frustrated and confused. As the meanness of their poverty-stricken surroundings took on the look and smell of an urban ghetto, desperation mounted, fears multiplied, and the air was filled with unanswered questions. Could a ghetto, with its crime, deprivation, and social disorganization actually develop within the very bosom of one of the world's most affluent cities? What were the chances for renewal of hope or escape from defeat? Could one grope his way out of the fog of squalor or was entrapment forever? These questions became Hughes's questions; and, as he wrote his poems, he began to speak with the many voices of Harlem's anxiety. As Arthur Davis states in "The Harlem of Langston Hughes' Poetry" (*Phylon*, 1952), by 1942, the year of the publication of *Shakespeare in Harlem*, "the black metropolis was a disillusioned city"—a "black city settled down to the drab existence of WPA and relief living." With the passing of the years, Harlem's situation worsened, and the voice of the poet in *One-Way Ticket* (1949) and *Montage of a Dream Deferred* (1951) reflected the city's decline.

An interesting prelude to the social, economic, and political concerns expressed in his poems about Harlem in the 1940s was Hughes's "Ballad of the Landlord," first published in *Opportunity* (Dec. 1940) and then included as one of the poems in *Jim Crow's Last Stand* (1943) and later in *Montage of a Dream Deferred*. In 1940, the poem was a rather innocuous rendering of an imaginary dialogue between a disgruntled tenant and a tight-fisted landlord. In creating a poem about two such social archetypes, the poet was by no means taking any new steps in dramatic poetry. The literature of most capitalist and noncapitalist societies often pits the haves against the have-nots, and not infrequently the haves are wealthy men of property who "lord" it over improvident men who own nothing. So the confrontation between tenant and landlord was in 1940 just another instance of the social malevolence of a system that punished the powerless and excused the powerful. In fact, Hughes's tone of dry irony throughout the poem leads one to suspect that the poet deliberately overstated a situation and that some sardonic humor was supposed to be squeezed out of the incident. Says the Tenant in furious high dudgeon:

What? You gonna get eviction orders?
You gonna cut off my heat?
You gonna take my furniture and
Throw it in the street?

Um-huh! You talking high and mighty.
Talk on—till you get through.
You ain't gonna be able to say a word
If I land my fist on you.

The Man of Property, in fear and trembling, invokes the symbols of law and order:

Police! Police!
Come and get this man!
He's trying to ruin the government
And overturn the land!

Ironically, this poem, which in 1940 depicted a highly probable incident in American urban life and was certainly not written to incite an economic revolt or promote social unrest, became, by the mid-1960s, a verboten assignment in a literature class in a Boston high school. In his Langston Hughes headnote in *Black Voices* (1967), Abraham Chapman reported that a Boston high school English teacher named Jonathan Kozol was fired for assigning it to his students. By the mid-sixties, Boston and many other American cities had become riot-torn, racial tinderboxes, and their ghettos seethed with tenant anger and discontent. So the poem gathered new meanings reflecting the times, and the word of its tenant persona bespoke the collective anger of thousands of black have-nots. In his review of Gwendolyn Brooks's *Street in Bronzeville* in *Opportunity* (Fall 1945), Hughes praised that young poet's initial volume of poems for its incisive social and political statements and for its "picture-power." His conclusion was that "Poets often say these things better than politicians." Such a comment aptly fits "Ballad of the Landlord." At least, someone on the Boston School Committee evidently thought so.

The publication of *Shakespeare in Harlem* announced to the literary world that Hughes had returned poetically to Harlem. After the somewhat frenetic international traveling of the 1930s and after the years of outspoken commitment to radical political and social causes, his literary homecoming was comparatively quiet. In fact, the poems in this volume reflect a return of the folk poet who had, as in the 1920s, prowled Harlem's streets to record his flitting impressions of the life-styles and racial postures and attitudes of Harlem's citizenry. But, as noted above, the Harlem of 1942 was vastly different from that of 1926. Even in the earlier Harlem, beneath its nightclub glitter, Hughes had heard a "jazz band sob." But in *Shakespeare in Harlem* unhappiness is omnipresent, especially in the two sections on Harlem—"Death in Harlem" and "Lenox Avenue." The happy hedonism of the 1920s is gone; all that remains is misery and sorrow. As Arthur Davis states in "The Harlem of Langston Hughes' Poetry,"

> There are no bright colors . . . only the sombre and realistic shades appropriate to the depiction of a community that has somehow lost its grip on things. The inhabitants of this new Harlem impress one as a beaten people.

Davis notes further that even the "night life world" had become cruel and stripped of the fun and illusion once associated with the finger-popping excitement of the night jazz centers of the twenties. Instead of having gay, high-kicking times at Dixie's place, the customers have to flee madly when a jealous and angry Arabella Johnson shoots down a warm and loving Bessie over a "cat" named Texas Kid. But this is the lot of Harlem lovers in *Shakespeare in Harlem*. In Davis's words, they "are an aggrieved lot"—frustrated and unfulfilled and "whining perpetually about being 'done wrong.' " The calculating cynicism of the pimp has replaced the tender loving concern of the lover. And the pimp's masochistic loved one, in desperation, vows:

> . . . I can't help lovin' you
> Though you do me wrong—
> But my love might turn into a knife
> Instead of to a song.

Inevitably, few critics found drinking from this full cup of poetic misery a pleasant task. Mary Colum, for instance, in her review in the *New York Times Book Review* (March 22, 1942), said that the poems in *Shakespeare in Harlem* depicted, in somewhat monotonous fashion, Harlemites who were "immensely sad, even hopeless." And she deplored the fact that, instead of dancing or laughing or singing for relief, Hughes's personae vented their griefs and anxieties by rushing "into some activity—love, . . . or fighting, gambling." Indeed, the absence of joy and happiness in this volume of poetry led the reviewer to an interesting and provocative conclusion—one that exactly countered the long-held stereotypical view of the happy, dancing Negro with a stereotype of her own. Wrote Ms. Colum:

> The Europeans seem to be the only branch of the human race who ever believed much in the joy of life or went in much for the praise of life.

In retrospect, it would seem that the grimness and misery of *Shakespeare in Harlem* caused at least one reviewer to forget that Europe produced the melancholy Dane and the Wagnerian Götterdammerung.

Other reviewers were similarly unenthusiastic, though for different reasons. Owen Dodson, writing for *Phylon* (Third Quarter, 1942), then under the aegis of its founding editor, W. E. B. Du Bois, assumed a predictably "talented tenth" attitude. Dodson wrote:

> Mr. Langston Shakespeare Hughes is still holding his mirror up to a gold-toothed flashy nature . . . somehow the glass is cracked and his deep insight and discipline has [sic] dimmed.

In another section of his review he likened the experience of reading the poems to seeing and hearing "a cartoon doing a black-face, white-lip number." Indeed, one of his interesting observations was that if one just sat and heard the poems read, he would conclude that "Langston Hughes must be a cracker." His conclusion was that *Shakespeare in Harlem* revealed a poet who "was backing into the future looking at the past."

Interestingly enough, in the year immediately preceding the appearance of Dodson's review, "Mr. Langston Shakespeare Hughes" had published a short article in *Phylon* (First Quarter, 1941) in which he sought to explain his attitude toward "Songs Called the Blues." From this short but pithy statement, one can infer what the poet was trying to do in *Shakespeare in Harlem*. First, he defined blues as "city songs rising from the crowded street of big towns." Second, the blues are songs "you sing alone," unlike spirituals which are "group songs." Third, blues are "folk songs born out of heartache." Fourth, whereas spirituals are "escape songs," the blues are "today songs, here-and-now, broke-and-broken hearted" songs. The poet concluded his short article with a brief cataloguing of the kinds of blues blacks had to sing in their urban ghettos: "Family Blues, Loveless Blues, Left-lonesome Blues, Broke-and-hungry Blues, and Desperate, Going-to-the-river Blues."

Although it is critically hazardous to attempt to define an author's intentions, Hughes's poems of sadness and misery in *Shakespeare in Harlem* become more meaningful if they are viewed as a pastiche of the big-city blues—songs "born out of heart-ache" and "rising from the crowded streets" of the black ghetto. In these poems, the poet's concern was not to tell about yesterday nor tomorrow, but to write those "today songs" of the "broke and broken-hearted" in the realistic "here-and-now." Inevitably, the picture of Harlem that emerged was appalling, especially to a nation that, in 1942, had already ventured forth to defend the four freedoms throughout the world. To Hughes's credit, it can now be said that in his slender volume he cited most of the causes that sparked Harlem's second riot in 1943. But then, as he had said of Gwendolyn Brooks, poets often say certain things better than politicians.

William Harrison's review of *Shakespeare in Harlem* in *Opportunity* (Feb. 1942) also ignored the fact that many of the poems in the volume could have developed from a Hughesian blueprint for black urban blues. The personae of the poems, Harrison complained, were all too often "the most uprooted . . . Negro social types." Did the poet have to concentrate on "the folk-experience of the Negro people" and emphasize "the depths of Negro life" and yet strike "no note of hope for the future"? In critical retrospect, the answer is clear: if the subject of *Shakespeare in Harlem* were black urban blues, Hughes had no choice but to write about those interactions of person and event that produced the blues.

By the time Hughes produced his next volume of poems about Harlem, many significant events had occurred on the black literary scene. First, Richard Wright wrote *Native Son* in 1940 and *Black Boy* in 1945 and stimulated a new wave in naturalistic black fiction that stressed strident protest against American racism. And Wright himself exercised his own right of protest by leaving America to accept self-imposed exile in France. Second, new literary figures were beginning to make their appearance—Gwendolyn Brooks in poetry, Ralph Ellison and Frank Yerby in fiction, and James Baldwin as an essayist and future novelist. The poet himself, impressed by the popular success of his Simple stories, was also leaning toward fiction as a medium for interpreting the black man's experience. But while on the high tide of post-World War II interest in the Negro's literature, he also began to busy himself producing anthologies and translations of poetry from the so-called Third World.

In 1949, he collaborated with Arna Bontemps on an anthology of *The Poetry of the Negro, 1746–1949*; and, between 1947 and 1951, he published translations of Roumain's *Master's of the Dew* (with Mercer Cook's assistance), Guillén's *Cuba Libre* (with Ben Carruthers's assistance), and Lorca's *Gypsy Ballads*. At this point, it is interesting to note that as Hughes broadened his literary scope and interests, the emerging new black writers, particularly those in fiction, concentrated with grim moral and sociological fury on that very ghetto which had been the poet's special subject for many years. Indeed, it is somewhat ironic that Hughes's long-time friend and fellow writer, Arna Bontemps, could report somewhat defensively in his article, "The Harlem Renaissance" (*Saturday Review*, March 22, 1947), that Hughes's most recent volume of poetry, *Fields of Wonder* (1947), "contains not a single blues note." It is obvious from the general tone of Bontemps's comments that he was quite happy to be able to make such a report although his report did not match the facts. Apparently, throughout the years he had been disturbed that Hughes's "preoccupation with low life, with the singers of blues, with rounders and cabaret girls, with the misery and exaltation of road workers and of shouting church folk" provoked such strong disapproval among the Negro middle class. For this reason, Arna Bontemps, friend and collaborator of many years, was immensely pleased that Hughes's appeared at long last to have turned away from the urban blues in *Fields of Wonder*.

It is now apparent that Bontemps was influenced less by his sound critical judgment than by his friendly concern for the literary reputation of a man with whom he had enjoyed such a rich and productive association for almost a quarter of a century. For, although there are no blues poems per se in the section of *Fields of Wonder* entitled "Stars of Harlem," Arthur Davis (1952) is quite right in stating that "The mood . . . continues in the sombre vein of *Shakespeare in Harlem*, and the idea of escape is stated or implied in each of the poems." The description of the trumpet player on Fifty-second Street, for instance, is not that of the happily creative jazzer of the 1920s. Rather, he "Has dark moons of weariness/ Beneath his eyes/Where the smoldering memory/Of slave ships/ Blazed to the crack of whips/About his thighs." The black man's music in this place and time is filled with bitter racial memories and the happy black minstrel dispensing laughter and joy is no more. And in "Dimout in Harlem" the images of shadow and silence prevail, for "dimout" is another word for the social and personal blight that has afflicted young Harlem:

> Down the street young Harlem
> In the dusk is walking
> In the dusky dimout
> Down the street is walking

Shadows veil his darkness
Shadows veiling shadows
Soft as dusk the darkness
Veiling shadows cut by laughter
Then a silence over laughter

Shadows veiling silence
Silence veiling shadows
Silence and the shadows
Veiling Harlem's laughter

But sometimes a poet needs a friend more than he needs a critic, and Arna Bontemps provided a warm tribute to Langston Hughes in "Negro Poets, Then and Now" (*Phylon* Fourth Quarter, 1950), devoted to the subject: "The Negro in Literature: The Current Scene." First, Bontemps gave his friend due praise for being "the only Negro poet since Dunbar who has succeeded in making a living from his poetry." Then, in a somewhat humorous tone, he explained the versatile uses of Hughes's poetry.

a poem must be used many ways to yield enough sustenance to keep a hearty individual like Mr. Hughes in the kind of food he likes. Therefore it is not surprising to find his poems being danced by Pearl Primus . . . sung by Juanita Hall . . . and recited by Paul Robeson in the United States and Central America.

Had Arna Bontemps had a crystal ball by which he could have foretold future literary events, he would have added that one of the lines from *Montage of a Dream Deferred* was to become the title of one of the great plays of the 1950s—*A Raisin in the Sun*. He might also have added that only rarely does a writer like Hughes appear—a writer who could effectively influence the work of so many other artists and cultural spokesmen in other genres and forms of artistic expression.

Hughes's next book of poetry on Harlem, *One-Way Ticket* (1949), was more specific than *Fields of Wonder* in revealing further nuances of the poet's "contre-temps of love" with Harlem. In a sense, the poem "Puzzled" summarizes the dilemma of Harlem's betrayed and bewildered citizenry and reflects the poet's own growing disenchantment:

> Here on the edge of hell
> Stands Harlem—
> Remembering the old lies,
> The old kicks in the back,
> The old, *Be patient*,
> They told us before.
> Sure, we remember. . . .
>
> We remember the job we never had,
> Never could get,
> And can't have now
> Because we're colored.
>
> So we stand here
> On the edge of hell
> In Harlem
> And look out on the world
> And wonder
> What we're gonna do
> In the face of
> What we remember.

Then in "Juice Joint: Northern City" the mood is even more depressed. Folks socialize and get "juiced," high, or drunk. But there is none of the hilarity that one found in "Dixie's Place" in some of the poems in the earlier *Shakespeare in Harlem* in 1942. In the poem "Juice Joint" some "forget to laugh who are still kids," and the closing lines describe "a slow, sad dance" when a

> . . . guitar-playing lad
> Whose languid lean brings back the sunny South
> Strikes up a tune all gay and bright and glad
> To keep the gall from biting in his mouth,
>
> > Then drowsy as the rain
> > Soft sad black feet
> > Dance in this juice joint
> > On the city street.

Gone are the happy dancing feet, the Bo-jangle bounce, the hand-clapping merriment. The ruthless city and its sprawling black ghetto have taken away all of the laughter and left only the "slow, sad dance" of "soft sad black feet."

Indeed, in the Harlem of *One-Way Ticket* even suicide is impossible, as the poem "Life Is Fine" demonstrates:

I went down down to the river
I sat down on the bank
I tried to think but couldn't
So I jumped in and sank. . . .

But it was
Cold in that water
It was cold!

I took the elevator
Sixteen floors above the ground
I thought about my baby
And I thought I would jump down. . . .

But it was
High up there!
It was high!

In the end, the poem's insecure *persona* decides to whistle his way by the graveyard of life by declaring:

Life is fine!
Fine as wine!
Life is fine!

Admittedly, there is a certain amount of wry humor in this portrait of the self-doubting and somewhat cowardly suicidist, but the last three lines echo the self-administered psychological narcotic which enabled Harlemites to survive on "the edge of Hell." Later, in "Junior Addict," one of the poems in Hughes's final volume *The Panther and the Lash* (1967), the narcotic used is no longer a symbol: here there is a "little boy" who, in his attempt to close out "Harlem screams," sticks a needle in his arm and then nods "in other wordly dreams." By the late 1960s, Harlem's "deferred dream" had turned into a surrealistic nightmare.

In his 1952 essay, Arthur Davis states that "the longest and most revealing Harlem poem in *One-Way Ticket* is the thumping 'Ballad of Margie Polite,' the Negro girl who 'cussed a cop . . . and caused a riot." Certainly, this poem does provide a convincing commentary on the hair-trigger sensitivities that spark riots in poverty-seared urban ghettos, and Hughes relates Margie Polite's story with considerable narrative skill and finesse. But in his 1968 essay "Langston Hughes: Cool Poet," Davis also gives deserving praise to the series of poems in *One-Way Ticket* entitled "Madam to You." These twelve short poems present Madam Alberta K. Johnson, a character who, like Jess B. Semple, was the product of Hughes's comic vision and, in Davis's view, "almost as great a creation as Simple." As the poet weaves through the light and shadow of the career of "this tough, intelligent and realistic lady," one gains a full appreciation of her survival power in Harlem's ever-challenging environment. There is a heart-warming and resilient independence about her as she gives her "comeuppance" to the various institutional representatives who so often beleaguer the urban poor: a landlord's agent, a somewhat nosy "Reverend Butler," a census taker, and a "lady from the Juvenile Court." Although her many economic misadventures would have defeated a less resourceful person, Madam proclaims to the world:

> DON'T WORRY ABOUT ME!
> Just like the song,
> . . . take care of yourself—
> And I'll get along.

Predictably, Madam's experiences with the men in her life ("I had two husbands/I could have had three") bred in her a certain cynicism, but there is something warmly human about her when she sends away "Jackson," her tender-loving "might-have-been," because

> When you think you got bread
> It's always a stone—
> Nobody loves nobody
> For yourself alone.

At the same time, Madam is a person of compassionate concern. During her lifetime, she has adopted and reared two "charity" children who were quickly "ruint" by the city's temptations. To her they were

> Poor little things
> Born behind the 8–rock,
> With parents that don't even
> Stop to take stock.

Finally, she believes in fortune-tellers and courts "lady luck" by playing the numbers. But life has prepared her to lose with good-humored grace:

> ... I swear I
> Ain't gonna play no more
> Till I get over
> To the other shore—
>
> Then I can play
> On them golden streets
> Where the number not only
> Comes out—but repeats!

From Harlem's busy, seething streets, Hughes presented many characters and types—lovers, pimps, harried wives, gamblers, and jazzing goodtimers—but no one is more appealing with her warmly flawed humanity than Madam Alberta K. Johnson.

Of the critics who commented on *One-Way Ticket,* only Arthur Davis perceives the link between an Alberta K. Johnson and a Jess B. Semple, but even he fails to elaborate on the full implications of Hughes's distinct gift for comic creativity. It is true that in his comments on what he calls the poet's "coolly ambivalent vision," this critic does identify the gift that enabled Hughes to objectify character and incident and present his short vignettes of dramatic realism. But Hughes was more than a poetic dramatist; he had a comic vision that enabled him to cover the pain and suffering of black urban existence with protective layers of wit, humor, and sympathetic understanding. The characters he presented are small, commonplace, and insignificant; they never charge up any Mount Everests nor do they live exciting or glamorous lives. They are error-ridden, often fearful, and yet filled with a good-humored acceptance of their own frailties. So in their small, unheroic ways they negotiate the complicated systems and bureaucracies burdening the black citizen in the biggest ghetto in America's largest city. This they do with a certain amount of bravado, a certain amount of humility, and a certain amount of good humor.

Apparently, Hughes was convinced that only people who have these qualities can survive "on the edge of Hell." He could have filled many books of poetry with accounts of the pitiful, stark tragedies that stalk the ghetto; but, had he done this, he would not have been able to stress what Stephen Henderson calls the "survival motion" of black people. Also Hughes may have realized that the so-called bottom line of the black man's ghetto existence will not be written by the "native son" who kills and is killed but by the Alberta K. Johnsons and Jess B. Semples who err and survive. This is not to say that Bigger Thomas's searing encounter with tragedy should never have been told. In many respects, that character was and is, as Wright said, America's metaphor. But in his emotional stature and grandeur of statement Bigger is the product of man's tragic vision. On the other hand, Hughes's folk vignettes are of much smaller dimension and thus have raised far lower decibels of critical praise. But, as products of the comic vision, they will continue to play enduring roles in man's social drama.

Unfortunately, Alain Locke, the one critic who, by virtue of his experience and breadth of literary interests, should have understood what Hughes was trying to say about life in Harlem, turned away from *One-Way Ticket* with something akin to disgust. In 1927, he had defended the poems in *Fine Clothes to the Jew* (*Saturday Review* April 9) because they presented "vivid, pulsing, creative portraits of Negro folk foibles and moods." But, by 1950, in his annual review of Negro literature for 1949 (*Phylon*, First Quarter) he had developed considerable distaste for the "glibly synthetic, one-dimensional folk vignettes" which he found in *One-Way Ticket*. Poets like Gwendolyn Brooks, Sam Allen, Owen Dodson, and Margaret Walker had created a new literary mood in black America; and Alain Locke thought that with a new and exciting decade of literary productivity in the offing, Hughes's poetry appeared sadly out of date. He did not explicitly charge, as Owen Dodson had earlier, that the poet "was backing into the future looking at the past." But he did condemn the poems of *One-Way Ticket* for their "facile superficiality" and issued this warning:

> Facility, undisturbed by fresh vision, can dim and tarnish almost any talent of whatever potential magnitude. Especially with the field of seriously experimental young contenders, Mr. Hughes, should he persist in his facile superficiality, will have to surrender his erstwhile cloak and laurels.

In retrospect, one can understand how a critic like Alain Locke would not, in 1950, be titillated by the comedy of ghetto life. A refined and cultured man of literature who had hovered over Negro literature for almost three decades, he was now in search of a literature of race that would leap over the bounds and limits of the urban black ghetto and become part of the American literary mainstream. In 1927 black ghetto folk had added an exotic excitement to the literary scene. Now in 1950 the literary air seemed to be alive with new promises, and in this new day Hughes's continued preoccupation with the comedy of the black ghetto seemed to Locke an unfortunate anachronism. Moreover, it is a reasonable assumption that a distinguished personage like Alain Locke, Negro America's first

Rhodes scholar, would find an aggressive matriarch like Madam
Alberta K. Johnson far more fearsome than instructive or entertaining.

The appearance of *Montage of a Dream Deferred* indicated that,
if Hughes had heard Locke's warning, he thought it literarily un-
feasible to accommodate the critic's aversion to poetizing folk vignettes from Harlem's ghetto. The unifying theme of a "dream
deferred" runs through most of the ninety poems in this volume;
but the poet, while inventorying the myriad ways in which Harlemites have their dreams "deferred," continued to be a random
observer with an essentially comic vision. For instance, he notes
"A woman standing in the doorway/Trying to make her where-
with-all" or a "night funeral in Harlem" at which a young man is
preached into his grave for a mere five dollars. From the ghetto's
human clutter also comes the wino

> Setting in the wine-house
> Soaking up a wine-souse
> Waiting for tomorrow to come—
> Then
> Setting in the wine-house
> Soaking up a new souse.
> Tomorrow . . .

Or there's the dancer who "tapped/boogied/sanded/jittered" but
"was no good at making love/and no good at making money." And
the poet notes the wife who alertly plays the number associated
with fish when her dying husband raises up from his deathbed and
asks for fish.

In addition, there are provocative dialogues in which Hughes,
with his "coolly ambivalent vision," gives both sides of an argument
between "low" folks and "high" folks about the Negro's racial
image or both sides of a discussion between mother and son about
sister's involvement with a married man. At other times, the poet
becomes a kind of ghetto spokesman giving forth small bits of
advice designed to help the collective "survival motion" of black
ghetto residents.

> Folks, I'm telling you,
> birthing is hard
> and dying is mean—
> so get yourself
> a little loving
> in between.

Or, as he observes,

> Cheap little rhymes
> A cheap little tune
> Are sometimes as dangerous
> As a sliver of the moon.
> A cheap little tune
> To cheap little rhymes
> Can cut a man's
> Throat sometimes.

The poet also feels a particular affinity for the "people of the night" who somehow have learned to "live and let live":

> Maybe it ain't right—
> but the people of the night
>   will give even
>   a snake
>   a break.

Many poems in *Montage* express the theme that Harlem's great afflictions are its "deferred" dreams and unfulfilled promises. As Wagner states in his discussion of *Montage*:

> the motif of the dream is . . . ubiquitous. . . . Like a flash of lightning it traverses the elements of this "montage," many of which amount to no more than a snatch of verse . . . it is not so much the dream itself as its reflection in the individual lives of countless Harlem dwellers that is offered us and, consequently, as something no less composite than life itself.

Wagner goes on to observe that actually "this dream is no longer something to be exalted, but a vision degraded through trampling, shoving, and abuse." Indeed, as Hughes says, Harlem's cluster of deferred dreams has become a time bomb hovering over the city and its people:

> What happens to a dream deferred?
>   Does it dry up
>   like a raisin in the sun?
>   Or fester like a sore—
>   And then run? . . .
>   *Or does it explode?*

Everywhere one looks in Harlem, there are deferred dreams. Some are large and important; some are relatively small and insignificant. For instance, in "Dime," when a tired, overworked Grandma is asked "lend me a dime" and "acts like/She ain't heard," her grandchild accepts her small deferred dream of the moment with "I might've knowed/It all the time." Then there are the larger deferred dreams of adult Harlem—the dream about "that white enamel stove" never purchased, the dream about studying French sometime, or buying a home, or passing a civil service exam, or taking up Bach. So pervasive are deferred dreams in Harlem that even Jewish storekeepers "shrug their shoulders" and say "What's the use/in Harlem?"—leading the poet to speculate:

> Sometimes I think
> Jews must have heard
> the music of a
> dream deferred.

One element in *Montage* that makes it distinctively different from its immediate predecessor, *One-Way Ticket*, is that the new jazz of the post-World War II period played a strong influence on the tone and structure of the poems. Wagner calls the poet's use of jazz in this volume "the most ambitious experiment undertaken by Hughes in this domain." Although this observation may come under question when one looks at the extensive jazz background of *Ask Your Mama* (1961), the poet did state his intention to provide in the many poems of *Montage* a composite jazz poem on contemporary Harlem. His objective was to have his montage of comments on Harlem reflect the spirit, quality, and tonality of the new jazz mode. His introductory statement is as follows:

> In terms of current Afro-American popular music and the sources from which it has progressed—jazz, ragtime, swing, blues, boogie-woogie, and be-bop—this poem on contemporary Harlem, like be-bop, is marked by conflicting changes, sudden nuances, sharp and impudent interjections, broken rhythms, and passages sometimes in the manner of a jam session, sometimes the popular song, punctuated by the riffs, runs, breaks, and distortions of the music of a community in transition.

Hughes's declaration of poetical purpose is in many ways a provocative statement which can lead one in many directions. In the first place, his poetry, from *The Weary Blues* on, had never been far removed from the black man's musical experience, with the possible exception of the leftist poetry he wrote during the 1930s. In those early days, he utilized the blues form, but only in a restricted sense did the forms of jazz actually influence the structure of his poetry at that time. The early poem "The Cat and the Saxaphone," for instance, was an experimental effort to structure a poem to fit a jazz medium. Generally, however, Hughes's so-called early jazz poems merely described some aspect of the impact of jazz on society. But the subject of the poet's use of form and structure is of much larger import than what he accomplished in his jazz and blues poetry. For in this context, one is also compelled to observe that although the poet used a traditional blues pattern in his early poems, he was, from the beginning, conscientiously nontraditional in matters of poetical structure and form. And it is also pertinent to observe that in his poetry form and structure always appeared to be subordinated in importance to meaning and message. Indeed, one is teased by the speculation that Hughes's apparent mode of poetical composition—the fashioning of a poem in an impromptu, impressionistic manner—may have actually precluded any sustained or meticulous attention to matters of style, form, and structure. Unfortunately, not enough hard evidence is available from Hughesian comment and criticism to raise this provocative speculation to the level of an unassailable critical conclusion. We do have Hughes's own account in *The Big Sea* (1940) of how, as a teenager, he composed "The Negro Speaks of Rivers" in an impromptu fashion while crossing the Mississippi River on a train trip to visit his father in Mexico. We also know that on occasion he "dashed off" angry poetical protests against some issue or event, but any additional evidence about the poet's mode of composition can only be adduced and inferred from the actual nature of most of his poetry. His poems are, as Blyden Jackson stated, in large measure a gleaning of impressions—at times insightful and penetrating and at other times trivial and casual. Hence, Hughes's poetry often lacks elaborate decorative imagery and weighty philosophical symbols. Clearly, this feature of his poetry alienated those critics who, like Wagner, tended to consider an impressionistic poetry which scorned traditional forms, style, and structure a poetry shallow in conception and small in emotional impact.

But all roads to poetical excellence are not necessarily lined with tradition and practices sanctified by time and authority. Happily, Hughes's gift for impromptu poetical improvisation found in the bebop jazz of the late 1940s and 1950s a stimulating and reenforcing cultural parallel. This new jazz style turned its back on traditional form and structure and emphasized each musician's right to improvise long solos with all of the technical skill and professional virtuosity he could muster at any given time. In such a musical environment, the group discipline, traditional with the big bands of the so-called swing era, was sacrificed to the skill of the individual performer. Forgotten was the need for a danceable beat or for music with audience appeal. To traditionalists like Louis Armstrong, the new jazz was an anathema which he labeled "the modern malice":

> you get all them weird chords which don't mean nothing and you got no melody to remember and no beat to dance to . . . and that's what that modern malice done for you.

But the practitioners of the art—Dizzy Gillespie, Miles Davis, Thelonious Monk, and Charlie "Yardbird" Parker—disagreed with Armstrong. They found that bebop, with its long, intricate solos and widely ranging improvisations, freed the Negro musician from the minstrel stigma. Not only did these musicians conscientiously ignore their audiences and the traditional structures and forms of jazz, but their music was a musician's music. Says Marshall Stearns in his *Story of Jazz*, "Ninths and augmented fourths (flatted fifths) became the cliches of bop, although they continued to sound like mistakes to the average Dixieland musician." The proper bebop soloist's stance was one of "hunched preoccupation" and "sonambulistic concentration"; and the music, shorn of any stated melody, ended whenever the soloist exhausted his instrumental inventiveness. Says Stearns:

> The bop soloist started and stopped at strange moments and places, reversing his breath pauses, and sometimes creating a long and unbalanced melodic line which cut across the usual rests.

But, in addition to bebop's emphasis on involved instrumental execution and its blatant disdain for traditional jazz form and structure, bebop also stressed that art and artists should be "cool." Apparently Hughes found all of these features of the new jazz fully compatible with his own musical and artistic tastes. He liked the bop musicians' flagrant disregard of the jazz conventions; he liked the way they fragmented melodic themes and improvised with an exciting kind of thematic discontinuity. He liked the way the artist imposed his mood and his manner on the forms of artistic expression.

Hence, his "Motto"—"I play it cool/And dig all jive"—a poem which not only reflects the persona's "cool" neutrality and marvelous self-possession in the face of it all, but mirrors as well the proper emotional stance of the bop musician who was coolly oblivious to everything except his own artistry. As the poet wrote in "Easy Boogie," he liked the musical mixture that blended "that steady beat" in the bass with the bebop soloist's "Riffs, smears, breaks." The net result was an earthy, "Hey-Lawdy-Mama" sexuality ("Easy like I rock it/In my bed!"). On another occasion, in "Boogie: 1 a.m.," "The boogie-woogie rumble/Of a dream deferred" appears in a fascinating musical mixture of trilling trebles and twining bass "Into midnight ruffles/Of cat-gut lace." Moreover, Hughes found the improvisational range of bebop exciting. Just as Charlie "Yardbird" Parker often could hear notes that he could not play until experimentation and execution carried him "to higher intervals of a chord as a melody line," so persons listening to bebop could discover hitherto unknown ranges of emotional response. In "Lady's Boogie" the poet wrote:

> See that lady
> Dressed so fine?
> She ain't got boogie-woogie
> On her mind—
>
> But if she was to listen
> I bet she'd hear
> Way up in the treble
> The tingle of a tear.
> *Be-Bach!*

There are also examples in *Montage* of the abrupt thematic changes so often practiced by bebop musicians. The initial poem, "Dream Boogie," actually conveys its message through the technique of thematic discontinuity. First, one hears the beat of "a boogie-woogie rumble," but there is an abrupt thematic change with the question

> *You think*
> *It's a happy beat?*
> Listen to it closely:
> Ain't you heard
> something underneath
> like a—

Then, the theme shifts again—

> *What did I say?*
> Sure,
> I'm happy!
> Take it away!

At this point sheer musicianship takes over, and the answers to the questions are lost in the double-treble "riffs, smears, and breaks" of soloing saxophone and trumpet.

Two other poems in *Montage* reflecting the influence of the bebop jazz mode are "Flatted Fifths" and "Dream Boogie: Variation." In both Hughes attempted to dig behind bebop's "cool" exterior for social and emotional meanings which related to the theme of the deferred dream. The message of "Flatted Fifths" seems to be that "Little cullud boys" wearing beards and berets and thus having the external markings of the "oop pop-a-da" bebopper are not in reality cool connoisseurs of the good life. Actually, they "horse a fantasy of days" and affect an elaborate facade by which they fool themselves into believing that their dreams are fulfilled and not deferred. They talk musician's talk about "flatted fifths," but it is all showy posturing. In the end, as potential draftees, they are in reality in flight from life "on the edge of hell." And the poet's use of the word "horse" might also signify how "little cullud boys" in berets effect a "cool" withdrawal from life's complexities through heroin or "horse," as this heavily used drug was called by Harlem's bebop generation. The poet also remarks on the fact that these young beboppers move from "flatted fifths" to "flatter beers," a line recalling traditional musician Eddie Condon's somewhat defensive response to the flatted-fifth emphasis in the bebop jazz style: "We don't flat our fifths; we drink 'em."

The second poem in which Hughes attempted to relate the deferred-dream theme to a musical experience is a short poem about a bebop organist who has

> High noon teeth
> In a midnight face,
> Great long fingers
> On great big hands.

With his size twelve shoe working on the "screaming pedals," he produces a sassily cool jazz that fascinates with its "tinkling treble" and "rolling bass." But behind the facade of musicianship and flawless execution, there lurks the shadow of a deferred dream:

> Looks like his eyes
> Are teasing pain
> A few minutes late
> For the Freedom Train.

Like the trumpeter on New York's Fifty-second Street whose weary eyes hold the "smoldering memory of slave ships," this superb organist cannot play away the "pain" of never having boarded America's "Freedom Train."

Of the critics who have commented specifically on *Montage* only Jean Wagner seems to appreciate that the slender volume of poems is in reality a "jam session" in poetry. The many voices that speak about the myriad ways in which Harlem's dreams are deferred are like instruments played by musicians who range over Harlem's experiences with a freedom authorized by their artistry. Writes Wagner:

> As in a jam session, this underlying theme [of the dream deferred] is first indicated . . . , then clearly stated, and then developed and picked up as each instrument in the band successively paraphrases it, weaves arabesques around it, and responds to one another.

Although he does not make specific mention of the influence of bebop jazz on the tone and structure of many of the poems in the collection, the French critic does note "the digressive introduction of incidental or conflicting themes." And the occasional "cavalier blending of the most elevated, serious themes" with those which "are utterly inept or banal" he attributes to "the temperamental quirks of the 'instrumentalists'" who are participating in this jam session of poetic comment. Wagner's general conclusion is that the "attempts to fuse jazz and poetry" in *Montage* are "interesting, praise-worthy technical experiments" which help to convey a "lively impression of the manifold . . . nuances of existence in . . . Harlem." His one *caveat*—and it is a sound one—is that sometimes the fusion of two media of artistic expression like jazz and poetry can tempt the artist to be less than vigilant about the artistic demands of both media. Or zeal for experimentation can at times force an artist to ignore the demands of one medium in deference to those of the so-called fusing medium. The net result says Wagner, can be "an overdone frivolousness" in poetic subject and style and an artistic product which is a disservice to both jazz and poetry. This is certainly true of certain poems in this volume. However, viewing Hughes's experimentation in *Montage* in the context of the somewhat exciting and revolutionary experiments then taking place in the jazz world, one can evaluate his attempts to fuse jazz and poetry with more sympathetic understanding. For bebop jazz sought to be cool, impartial, and stoically ambivalent about Harlem's deferred dreams and Harlem's persistent misery. In other words, to use the language of modern communication theory, the message was not the medium nor the medium the message; but the manner and style of the medium influenced both the impact of the message and the emotional and psychological release of the instrumentalist or artist who delivered the message. Proof of the impact of the poet's message throughout America and the world was the tremendous success of Lorraine Hansberry's *A Raisin in the Sun*, a powerful drama on the deferred dreams of a typical black urban family—a play based on an idea contained in one line in "Harlem," one of the poems in *Montage*.

In general, Alain Locke's comments on *Montage*, written a decade earlier than those by Jean Wagner, have the same critical thrust. Writing in *Phylon* in his annual review of literature for Negroes in 1951 (First Quarter, 1952), Locke hails *Montage* as

> a golden title and a potential bonanza of the Negro's urban frustration moods. Here is a subject and a poet made for each other and here and there are occasional glints of this gifted poet's golden talent.

But, like Wagner, the American critic feels that Hughes's performance was seriously marred by his persistent tendency to mix the frivolous and the trivial with the serious and the perceptive. There is altogether too much "flip doggerel" ("Daddy/don't let your dog/curb you!"). The unfortunate result is, in Locke's view, a general "unevenness of artistic conception." However, where Wagner attributes the unfortunate admixture of the frivolous and the serious to Hughes's zeal for experimentation in fusing jazz and poetry, Locke identifies no specific cause but ascribes it to a persistent weakness in Hughes's artistry and craftsmanship as a writer. This is revealed in his comments on *Laughing to Keep from Crying*, Hughes's collection of short stories which Locke discussed in his review of Negro literature for 1952 (*Phylon* First Quarter, 1953). Here again he deplores Hughes's "uneven writing," terming it "typical Langston Hughes"—full of "flashes of genius, epigrammatic insight" but impaired by a "tantalizing lack of follow-through"—"dish-water—and then suddenly crystal springs." One wonders if Locke would have arrived at the same critical conclusion about *Montage* if he had examined the poems within the context of jazz-poetry experimentation. The probable answer is that he would still have perceived Hughes as a "carelessly tipsy laureate" who dared to appear in print with "his laurel askew." For in this distinguished critic's view, the mode and method of black ghetto jazz would have contaminated and not enhanced poetic expression. Alain Locke never completely divested himself of his "talented tenth" perspective.

Regrettably, the message of *Montage* was completely lost upon Babette Deutsch who, in an article entitled "Waste Land of Harlem," reviewed the volume for the *New York Times Book Review* (May 6, 1951). All this poet-reviewer saw in the poems was a "kind of contrived naivete" and a "facile sentimentalism that stifles real feeling with a cheap scent." Indeed, it was her studied conclusion that *Montage* sounded the death knell of poetry based on "folk art." Actually, Hughes was sounding the death knell of the American city in a medium dictated by the times. That once again his artistic intentions were misread and misunderstood certainly did not surprise, disillusion, nor discourage him. An appraisal and evaluation of his work from the early 1950s to his death in 1967 will reveal that he kept both his verve and nerve as a functioning poet, interpreting urban life during America's most calamitous mid-century decades.

References

Bontemps, Arna
1947. "The Harlem Renaissance," *Saturday Review of Literature* March 22, pp. 12–13, 44.
1950. "Negro Poets, Then and Now," *Phylon* Fourth Quarter, pp. 335–60.
Chapman, Abraham
1968. (editor) *Black Voices.* New York: New Amer. Lib.
Colum, Mary
1942. "Review of *Shakespeare in Harlem*," *New York Times Book Review* March 22, p. 2.
Davis, Arthur
1952. "The Harlem of Langston Hughes' Poetry," *Phylon* 13:276–83.
1968. "Langston Hughes: Cool Poet," *CLA Journal June*, pp. 280–96.
Deutsch, Babette
1951. "Wasteland of Harlem," *New York Times Book Review* May 6, p. 23.

Dodson, Owen
  1942. "Review of *Shakespeare in Harlem*," *Phylon* Third Quarter,
  pp. 337–38.
Gibson, Donald
  1973. (editor) *Modern Black Poets*. New York: Prentice-Hall.
Harrison, William
  1942. "Review of *Shakespeare in Harlem*," *Opportunity* July,
  p. 219.
Hughes, Langston
  1941. "Songs Called the Blues," *Phylon* First Quarter, pp. 143–45.
  1945. "Review of *Streets of Bronzeville*," *Opportunity* Oct., p. 222.
Locke, Alain
  1950. "Annual Review of Negro Literature—1949," *Phylon* First
  Quarter, pp. 5–12.
  1952. "Annual Review of Negro Literature—1951," *Phylon* First
  Quarter, pp. 7–18.
  1953. "Annual Review of Negro Literature—1952," *Phylon* First
  Quarter, pp. 34–44.
Wagner, Jean
  1962. *Les Poètes Nègres des États-Unis*. Paris: Librairie Ista.

CHAPTER 5

Requiem for
"A Dream Deferred"

Following the publication of *Montage of a Dream Deferred* in 1951, the literary career of Langston Hughes turned from poetry and Harlem to other areas of literary concern which, in turn, occasionally demanded new and different modes of expression. In the early 1950s, America was still in the cold-war aftermath of the war of the previous decade, but international political tensions apparently had no adverse effect on Hughes's high rate of literary productivity. In fact, because the 1950s were marked both by the incipient decline of African and Caribbean colonialism and by the emergence of an invigorating group of new Afro-American writers, the Harlem poet found the decade to be one of the most productive of his entire literary career. He had long been concerned about "Africa imprisoned/In her bitter sorrow" and knew well that colonialized continent's travail and woe. Now, with Britain's gradual withdrawal from its colonial commitments and the emergence of Ghana and Nigeria as independent states, the poet rejoiced to note that Africa, the world's "sleeping giant," was beginning to awaken. And, at the end of the decade, he hailed the new Africa with these lines:

> Now I see the thunder
> And the lightning
> In your smile.
> Now I see
> The storm clouds
> In your waking eyes:
> The thunder
> The wonder
> And the young
> Surprise.

Freedom was not only astir in Africa; after the lapse of 150 years since Haitian independence, the islands of the Caribbean began to shake off the yoke of colonialism. On these islands were the "black seed" of Africa's sons and daughters who, in the 1950s, began to be aware of a close ethnic kinship with inhabitants of the "mother continent." Hughes and others had noted in the 1930s that there were firm cultural ties linking all black people to African roots; he and others also believed that, contrary to general belief, enslavement and other imposed cultural differences had not obliterated the African heritage. Indeed, in 1939, Senghor from Senegal, Césaire from Martinique, and Damas from French Guinea (now Guyana) had developed the concept of *Négritude* to describe the cultural unity of black people. At the same time Hughes had stressed that oppression, poverty, and exploitation forced all black people into a kind of defensive unity which in turn reenforced that cultural unity. Now in the 1950s a black economic and cultural cohesiveness began to be felt throughout the world community; and, in response to these new developments, Hughes began to edit, translate, and comment upon the literature of the black diaspora. He had long been an adherent of *Négritude;* he now became its articulate spokesman and literary practitioner.

The poet also found events and developments in Afro-American literature during the 1950s immensely stimulating. Although Richard Wright had joined the colony of American expatriates in Paris, he and Hughes continued to enjoy an amicable literary friendship that had begun in 1934 when, according to Arna Bontemps, Hughes came to Chicago from Carmel, California, for the express purpose of getting to know "this Richard Wright who's writing for the *Masses.*" At that time Wright was, in Bontemps's words, "a flaming young Communist" who preferred political discussion to dancing and girls; and at that time, Hughes, recently returned from Russia, was similarly inflamed with a passion for leftist causes. The Harlem poet also knew and befriended many of the younger black writers who had begun to publish during the 1940s and early 1950s. Foremost among these new young writers was Gwendolyn Brooks whose initial work, *A Street in Bronzeville*, had been favorably reviewed by Hughes in 1945. Later, in her autobiography, *Part One*, she described a party that she and her husband gave for Langston Hughes during those years of bright excitement and literary effervescence right after World War II. She had these words of tribute to a dear friend and kind sponsor:

> Langston Hughes loved literature. He loved it not fearfully, not with awe. His respect for it was never stiff nor cold. His respect for it was gaily deferential. He considered literature

not his private inch, but great acreage. The planting of others he not only welcomed but busily enriched. He had an affectionate interest in those young writers. . . . The young manuscript-bearing applicant never felt himself an intruder, never went away with Oak turned ashes in the hand.

In the same context, Gwendolyn Brooks also described the Harlem poet's "colloquial" conviviality and his racially reverent propensity for "mustard greens, ham hocks, and candied sweet potatoes."

There were other young and emerging writers who found Hughes helpful and encouraging. Owen Dodson, for instance, despite an early somewhat demeaning review of *Shakespeare in Harlem*, remembers him kindly as a person who had "a beautiful perception about people" and was determined to stay on Harlem's 127th Street and grow flowers in the ghetto. Similarly, Lorraine Hansberry and Margaret Walker valued Hughes's friendship. The former, whose play *Raisin in the Sun* became a stellar production of the 1950s, was stimulated by Hughes to take a line from one of his poems and forge it into a Broadway winner. Margaret Walker, in a *Phylon* article on "New Poets" in 1950, cited the Harlem poet as a model for all younger poets, because he had introduced into black poetry the significantly new "idiom of the blues." By so doing, Hughes had pierced the wall between intraracial classes and helped to create a sense of racial community. All later black poets, said Walker, were to benefit from Hughes's introduction of secular folk motifs into black poetry.

However, between Hughes and James Baldwin, another young writer with a rapidly escalating reputation in the 1950s, relationships were not always mutually supportive. In the first place, Baldwin's essay, "Everybody's Protest Novel," published in *Partisan Review* in 1949, displeased all black writers who, like Hughes, had protested long and vigorously against racial inequities. In his essay, Baldwin had placed black protest fiction in the same literary pigeonhole reserved for that classic of nineteenth-century abolitionist fiction, *Uncle Tom's Cabin*. Undoubtedly, the young essayist's somewhat brazen critical ploy of associating the strong naturalistic fiction of a Richard Wright with the sentimentalized moralizing of a Harriet Beecher Stowe was not without pejorative intent. Moreover, there was more than a little sarcastic needling in Baldwin's implication that a peculiar kind of "Uncle Tomism" colored all protest fiction. Inevitably, some of the more sensitive writers of black protest suspected that Baldwin's essay was intended to curry favor with the white literary establishment.

There is no evidence that Hughes joined those who leveled this somewhat invidious charge against Baldwin, but there is evidence that he neither forgot nor forgave the younger writer for his literary apostasy in attacking black protest fiction. In 1961, while serving on a radio panel with Alfred Kazin, Nat Hentoff, Baldwin, and others, Hughes, in response to Kazin's glowing praise of Baldwin's *Notes of a Native Son,* commented with malice aforethought that the book merited the highest critical tribute because it was "the *Uncle Tom's Cabin* of today." Earlier in that same panel discussion, Hughes had observed that Baldwin had some problems of cultural and racial identification and noted further that the younger writer could be "one of the most racial of our writers, in spite of his analysis of himself as otherwise on occasion." Baldwin's response to this gentle critical jab was not an extended statement of self-defense but a simple "Later for you." Actually, Hughes had made essentially the same observation about Baldwin's confusion about his cultural and racial identity in his review of *Notes of a Native Son* in 1956 ("From Harlem to Paris," *New York Times Book Review* Feb. 26, 1956). Not only did the older writer express the view that the young essayist was "quite a ways off" from being a genuine master of the written word, but he was also, in Hughes's opinion, too much "half American and half Afro-American" to have a clear-cut racial identity. Hughes concluded that once Baldwin extricated himself from his racial and cultural no-man's-land, he would write "with an illuminating intensity" that could "influence for the better all who ponder on the things books say." There is no evidence that the older writer ever came to believe that the younger writer fully solved his racial identity problems. On the other hand, there is considerable evidence that Baldwin thought that Hughes never fully solved his own limitations as a poet. The full extent of the younger writer's critical disenchantment with the older writer will be examined below when Baldwin's review of Hughes's *Selected Poems* (1959) is considered.

But during the 1950s his somewhat mild literary contretemps with Baldwin was an exception rather than the rule. Surrounded by an ever expanding coterie of literary friends and associates, and obviously stimulated by an ever broadening aura of literary good will, the poet not only published one or more books every year during the decade of the fifties, but his books began to enjoy a truly international exposure. His *First Book of Jazz,* for instance, originally published in New York in 1955, was, by 1960, published in five languages—Arabic, French, Japanese, Yugoslavian, and German. Similarly, *Famous American Negroes* (1954), went through various editions: Arabic, Brazilian, Pakistani, and three Indian editions. In general, Hughes's publications during the final fifteen years of his life (1952–67) reflected two major emphases. First, in several books —*Famous Negro Music-Makers* (1955), *First Book of Jazz, Famous Negro Heroes of America* (1958)—he wrote with spirit and fervor about black Americans, giving to a world of many colors and races a full view of America's largest and most troubled minority, even as Martin Luther King's program of nonviolent social change was beginning to affect and change basic patterns of racial relations in America. A second emphasis was on books stressing the growing cultural unity of black societies in Africa, the Caribbean, and Latin America. Examples of this emphasis are *The First Book of the West Indies* (1956), *First Book of Africa* (1960), and such anthologies as *An African Treasury* (1960) and *Poems from Black Africa, Ethiopia, and Other Countries* (1963).

In general, during his hardworking final decade and a half, Hughes's major medium was prose, with the exception of *Simply Heavenly* (1957)—a musical comedy version of the novel *Simple Takes a Wife*—and three volumes of poetry—*Selected Poems, Ask Your Mama* (1961), and *The Panther and the Lash* (1967). Admittedly, the large amount of fiction and history and the continuing emphasis on the Simple stories tended to reduce Hughes's status and role as a poet during his final years. But, lest the literary public forget that he had started his writing career as a poet and had written with verve and nerve for almost four decades, he published his *Selected Poems* in 1959. Just the year before he had published *The Langston Hughes Reader*, containing the literary bits and pieces of an extremely versatile career—some fiction, some drama, some autobiography, all of the poems from *Montage*, and some poems translated from the Spanish and from the French. So *Selected Poems* was designed to keep the career summary going, giving greater visibility and renewed vitality to the poems of the 1920s, 1930s, and 1940s.

The publication of this volume of poetry was a significant event in Afro-American literary history, for it marked only the second time that a black poet had selected his literary best for publication during his own lifetime. In 1947, Countee Cullen had published *On These I Stand*, and the reaction to this slim volume indicated that even the publication of one's best was not without some risk to one's literary reputation. Alain Locke's comment on Cullen's effort, for instance, was that the appearance of this poet's best was just another reminder of a poetical talent that "was prematurely dimmed and now regrettably lost." On the other hand, much earlier in the black man's literary history, the poetical works of two other famous poets had been collected for posthumous publication with generally good results. Phillis Wheatley's poems were collected and published together with a memoir of the poet in 1835, and Paul Lawrence Dunbar's poems were collected and published in 1913. These posthumous collections helped to reconfirm the high literary reputations both poets had enjoyed during their active literary careers. Unfortunately, historical precedents of this kind probably provided Hughes little comfort or counsel. For he must have realized that, as he pondered the somewhat momentous decision to collect and publish a selection of his poetry, his situation was far removed from that of a Wheatley or a Dunbar and even more risky than that of a Cullen. In the first place, as this study suggests, Hughes's relationships with his critics had not always been good, and the appearance of his "select best" could conceivably ignite old, long smoldering resentments. Then, too, there was another cause for concern. Over the decades, many things had changed, including literary styles and interests. So his projected volume faced a large new audience that might prove to be hostile or indifferent. It is plausible that to many persons in 1959 Hughes's approach to urban blues—his use of comic "jive" and the street-corner patois of the black ghetto—was as dated and as unpalatable as Dunbar's use of plantation dialect or Wheatley's use of eighteenth-century diction and imagery.

The man chosen to review *Selected Poems* for the *New York Times Book Review* was James Baldwin who, by the late 1950s, was well launched on a solid literary career as an essayist and novelist. Although a person of broad literary interests, Baldwin was not a poet. However, it should be immediately pointed out that this fact did not impair his ability to review a volume of poetry. Indeed, many nonpoets from DuBose Heyward in the 1920s down to David Daiches in the 1940s had reviewed Hughes's poetry with compassion and understanding. Rather, as has been suggested above, there may have been other reasons for the degree of incompatibility which existed between reviewer and reviewee. First, Baldwin and Hughes, although linked to each other by race and literary popularity, came from two vastly different literary worlds. The Harlem described in Hughes's poetry was not the Harlem that Baldwin knew. To the latter, Harlem was a gray pit of deprivation and not the glittering "jazzonia" that Langston had known early in his career. Moreover, this young novelist, as Keneth Kinnamon points out in his introduction to his edition of *Critical Essays on Baldwin* (Prentice-Hall, 1974), was "obsessively concerned with the writer's responsibility to save the world." For this reason, he was doubtless

suspicious of both Hughes's manner and matter. How can one ex-
tract humor and tolerant laughter out of black misery? How can
one find moral meaning in the innocuous comment and self-relieving
laughter of one-dimensional folk characters? Given the tragic pattern of interracial conflict in America, how can one justify the
comic celebration of the urban black life-style or justify the depiction of a Madam Alberta K. Johnson or a Jesse B. Semple? Can even
a good poet "save the world" by writing about jazz, blues, and low-
down folks? Let it be quickly stated that there is no record that
Baldwin asked himself these questions as he sat down to review
Selected Poems, but one can speculate with some plausibility that
the review he finally wrote was motivated by a search for answers
to such questions.

One may also justifiably speculate that there were at least two
other points of incompatibility between reviewer and reviewee.
First, Hughes was twenty-two years older than Baldwin, and generation gaps of this kind can be significant. The older writer had
published two volumes of poetry and a novel before the younger
writer had attained his tenth birthday. Second, because of what
Kinnamon calls Baldwin's "relentless hatred" for his "tyrannical
and paranoid" stepfather, the novelist probably had difficulty with
ostensible substitute father figures. Whether this in any way seasoned the reviewer's attitude and blunted his critical objectivity one
cannot say. All that can be reliably stated is that Baldwin's review
of *Selected Poems* was one of the most disparaging and negative
critical appraisals ever accorded Hughes's poetry.

It was not a long review, although, conceivably, the careful appraisal of forty years of poetry, divided into thirteen subject-matter
groupings, could have merited both intensive and extensive critical
treatment. But Baldwin dismissed almost all of the three hundred
pages of poetry as material that "a more disciplined poet" would
have consigned to the wastebasket. He was particularly disenchanted
with the final section of the volume, "Words Like Freedom," which
he found to be filled with a "fake simplicity" that failed to communicate "the very difficult simplicity of experience." He also found it
regrettable that Hughes, after long years of authorship under less
than ideal circumstances, had been unable to resolve the conflict between a writer's "social and artistic responsibilities." Baldwin felt
that the maintenance of a neat distinction between the two was very
important for the black writer who would be successful. As for
Hughes's wide and effective use of the dramatic monologue, the
reviewer's only comment was that the poet had not yet mastered
"the poetic trick" of being "within experience and outside it at the

same time." How one masters such a "trick" Baldwin did not say
Nor was he at all pleased with the poet's effort to use the language
of the urban black ghetto. How and why he considered it defective
he did not say. Finally, Baldwin, after the manner of some of the
"talented tenth" reviewers of the 1920s, rejected Hughes's blues
poetry, although obviously not for the same reason. The early critics
thought that the blues were an affront to racial respectability. Baldwin thought that the blues resulted in a kind of socially negative
navel-gazing that would never help in effecting the kind of meaningful social change that would "save the world."

There is no record that Hughes ever replied to this review. Undoubtedly, had he been younger and had he had more time from his
extensive literary commitments, he might have replied to his critics
as he had done in his 1926 essay, "The Negro Artist and the Racial
Mountain." However, Baldwin's review did not go unchallenged.
Lloyd L. Brown, an associate editor of *Masses and Mainstream* and
one who was, in the words of Harold Cruse, "the official Negro
Communist-line man on Negro literature," responded approxi-
mately two months after the review to Baldwin in a May 24 letter
to the *Times Book Review*. Brown's sympathies and prejudices
were obvious. First, he defended Hughes in glowing terms as the
"poet laureate of our people"—one who had the "rare genius" to
speak for "the very heart of the Negro in America." Next, he questioned Baldwin's "qualifications" as "a critic of poetry." Nowhere,
in Brown's opinion, was there any evidence of Baldwin's proven
competence as a critic of poetry. Rather, the latter's province was
not criticism at all but a somewhat counterproductive preoccupation with "hurling spitballs at Negro Literature." Then, Brown
dealt Baldwin "the most unkindest cut of all" when he asserted that
the young novelist was disqualified to comment on Hughes because
he, Baldwin, belonged to a small group of "alienated Negro writers"
who believed that a Negro writer had to "write white" and remain
separated from his people. It is obvious that Baldwin deserved no
such canard; he had not written a "white" essay; he was merely disenchanted with most of Hughes's poetry in *Selected Poems*, and he
had exercised his right to express his disenchantment. In attacking
Baldwin on the score of racial loyalty, Brown touched on a matter
which was totally extraneous to the principal issue. The major weakness in Baldwin's review is that it contained little or no reference to
Hughes's craftsmanship as a poet. There was no analysis of how the
poems are made—no mention of the rich variety of approaches used
by Hughes—no mention of his imagery and the language employed
to make the imagery effective and meaningful. In other words,

Baldwin failed to examine the poet on the grounds of his poetic competence. Consequently, his criticism was as ineffective as the criticism of an earlier date when Hughes was indicted for using subject matter which, in the opinion of those early critics, did not support the cause of racial uplift and racial self-respect.

Other reviews of *Selected Poems* were similarly lacking in substantive critical analysis. Henry Winslow's review in the *Crisis* (Oct. 1959) contained no comment on Hughes's technical competence as a poet and no effective analysis of any portion of his poetry. Rather, the poet was praised for his "enduring exuberance" and for his thirty-five-year-long association with *Crisis*. Principally, Winslow resorted to bland generalizing. For instance, he found in Hughes's poems "words of wisdom rather than a wisdom of words." Or he observed that in these poems the poet's "subjects are not his objects"—a somewhat puzzling observation when coupled with the comment that most of the subjects of Hughes's poetry were black urbanites disillusioned by their "deferred" dreams.

Similarly, Alvaro Cardone-Hine's review in *Mainstream* (July 1959) was full of laudatory ad hominem generalizations: Hughes is hailed as "that warm world-wide sightseer in depth" and his volume of poems as "a limpid congregation of effortless rhyme and folk-like simplicity." The poems treat the "whole of the black man's world" and are not, to the reviewer's immense satisfaction, marred by "conventional morality" nor by the "intellectual strutting" found in most modern poetry. But Cardone-Hine abandoned this effusively laudatory tone in his criticism of the last section of *Selected Poems*, "Words like Freedom." In his opinion, the poems in this section deal too much with the abstract, and Hughes was not the kind of "rhetorical poet" who could "sustain a long abstract poem." Since "poetry cannot exist apart from the concrete," these abstract poems on freedom, in Cardone-Hine's view, probably should never have been attempted or certainly never published. Whether this opinion reflected the reviewer's political bias or a poorly buttressed literary or poetic theory is not revealed in the review essay.

Certainly other critics—Blyden Jackson, George Kent, and Jean Wagner—share the opinion that Hughes did not customarily write long poems well because he could not sustain the poetic mood. And they also share the view that his poetic forte was the short poem that communicates a sharp, concrete impression of an event or of a person. But all three of these critics would dissent from the view suggested by Cardone-Hine that Hughes's preoccupation with the concrete automatically implied an inability to write competent and acceptable poetry on abstract themes. Indeed, it can be demonstrated that the poet often used the concrete to document the abstract. For instance, the poems in *Montage* all supply hard and irrefutable evidence that America had failed, in Harlem at least, to adhere to the abstract principles of justice and equality for all. For this reason, black Harlem was full of deferred and not fulfilled dreams. Then, too, he had written several good short poems earlier in his career on abstract topics like justice, history, time, and the like. The critical conclusion that somehow eluded Cardone-Hine is that Hughes's poems of concrete incident provide a collective comment on the viability or nonviability of some abstract principle. As will be seen below, in *The Panther and the Lash* the poet actually juxtaposed abstract poems with poems of concrete incident when they had a mutual relevance for the same general theme. In other words, Cardone-Hine is incorrect in his assumption that Hughes had no competence in writing poetry on abstract themes.

In similar fashion, John Parker's review of *Selected Poems* (*Phylon*, Summer 1959) provides no new insights on the poems which represented almost forty years of literary productivity. This reviewer does raise a slight critical eyebrow over the book's organization; for the poems are grouped into thirteen sections in accordance with themes addressed and moods provoked, with no attention to order of composition or chronology. But it is difficult for Parker to squeeze any profound critical comment out of this fact; so, in the end, he too resorts to bland and innocuous generalizing. In Parker's view Hughes is a "lyricist of keen sensitivity and insight" and his poems reflect "the turbulent inner life of Brown Americans in their struggle to outdistance their social milieux."

In summary, like Winslow and Cardone-Hine, Parker's comments on *Selected Poems* are essentially without critical bite. On the other hand, Baldwin's comments are full of bite but unfortunately devoid of critical insight. The critical observations of the above might have been substantially improved had they at least highlighted some of the poet's extended use of technical experimentation as James Emanuel was to do later in his essay on "The Literary Experiments of Langston Hughes." Emanuel points out that Hughes took full advantage of almost every extant stylistic poetical innovation. Not only did he write poems like "Jitney" which are topological in conception, but he experimented with emblematic verse forms and poems full of newspaper headlines ("Ballad of the Landlord") or poems in which a medley of miscellaneous voices chant a single theme ("Montage of a Dream Deferred"). In the final analysis, whatever is said about critical reactions to the volume, it must be remembered that *Selected Poems* was essentially a summary collection of a poet's best. Thus, the volume was for many old wine in old bottles. That the poet could produce a sparkling new vintage was proven with the publication of *Ask Your Mama*.

Ask Your Mama was Langston Hughes's tenth volume of poetry and, according to listings in Dickinson's *Bio-bibliography*, Hughes's thirty-ninth publication. Published on the eve of his sixtieth birthday, this volume of poetry communicated to Hughes's wide literary audience that not only was he live and hearty practically speaking, but he could participate with enthusiastic vigor in avant-garde literary ventures. For *Ask Your Mama* was part of a *nouvelle vague* in poetry which united the poet and the jazz musician as mutual folk spokesmen. Hughes had, from the beginning, celebrated jazz and blues in his poetry, and in *Montage* he had utilized the techniques and esthetic stance of the bebop style. By 1961, however, with the flowering of the "beat generation," the marriage of jazz and poetry became an accepted social and cultural fact and not just an isolated esoteric phenomenon for the delectation of selected literary dilettantes. With the appearance of writers like Ginsberg, Rexroth, and Kerouac, the emphasis on cool detachment and artistic aloofness gave way to an emphasis on various modes and levels of alienation, ranging from violent rejection of accepted social and moral norms to a frenzied search for an existential freedom that would leave one completely unencumbered by clan, kin, or country. In actuality, the beatnik was a psychological and emotional dropout from society and its folkways and, as such, represented a sort of delayed reaction to the excessive moral and patriotic commitments demanded of all of the major societies of the West during World War II. All things such as family, home, church, marriage, social status and position—all the things men, women, and children had suffered and died for and which had been excessively revered during the prolonged conflict—came to be scorned by a disputatious and disenchanted new generation. Not only were beatniks deaf to any kind of patriotic appeal, but they were disdainful of standard and traditional ways of maintaining law and order. In their view the effort to maintain law and order frequently frustrated any effort to effect meaningful social change.

Inevitably, poets became involved in the churning conflict between old and young. Many years before, T. S. Eliot, with fine prophetic insight, had predicted that within a short time "the darkness shall be the light and the stillness the dancing" and that the world would necessarily have to seek for new definitions. Until these new definitions were discovered and articulated in our society, "the faith and the love and the hope" would all be "in the waiting."

When, in the 1950s and early 1960s, what had been predicted by Eliot had indeed become a fact, poets led the way in trying to restore faith, hope, and love. To do this they reassumed a long-lost troubadour function, taking their poetry to the marketplace and to the open forum. And because they were artists speaking for and to the folk, quite often they were accompanied by musicians who also had a folk message about the restoration of faith, hope, and love. Kenneth Rexroth (*Nation*, 1958), one of the participating poets in the movement, describes how jazz blended with poetry when a poet declaimed his verses before a public audience:

> What is jazz poetry? It isn't anything very complicated to understand. It is the reciting of suitable poetry with the music of a jazz band, usually small and very quiet. Most emphatically, it is not recitation with "background" music. The voice is integrally wedded to the music and, although it does not sing notes, is treated as another instrument, with its own solos and ensemble passages, and with solo and ensemble work by the band alone.

Rexroth's brief definition omits mention of three important facts about jazz poetry. First, the poetry delivered before the people was usually a poetry strident with protest against the conventional and the traditional—a poetry often explicitly vulgar and disdainful of all long-accepted moral and social codes. Second, blending the voice of poetry with other musical instruments inevitably affected the quality and kind of poetry used in such public programs. The poet no longer reserved the right to communicate only with himself; internal dialogues or long contemplative mood-lyrics could not be used; communication had to be direct and the subject matter of broad public interest. Third, poetry could no longer have a traditional form, with traditional lines, traditional word patterns, or traditionally decorative imagery. If the music were brightly innovational and improvisational in theme and idea, the poetical voice had to be similarly free to innovate and improvise.

Hughes's *Ask Your Mama* conforms in many respects to this concept of jazz poetry. Throughout the twelve sections of the volume there are elaborate notes calling for the reciprocal interplay of music and poetry. The dominant theme that in "the Quarter of the Negroes" life is full of waiting and hesitating is stressed musically by "The Hesitation Blues," an old blues number used as a recurring leitmotif throughout *Ask Your Mama*. Moreover, the ringing indictments of social and moral injustice customarily found in the usual jazz poem are in full evidence in the volume. These are delivered with that peculiar Hughesian blend of anger, irony, and humor. For instance, all three emotions lurk behind these lines:

> Santa Claus, forgive me,
> But babies born in shadows
> In the shadow of the welfare
> If born premature
> Bring welfare checks much sooner
> Yet no presents down the chimney

Then, after the manner of the improvising musical soloist, the theme of "chocolate babies" born "in the shadow of the welfare" is elaborated upon and expanded and infused with provocative new meanings. The birth of welfare babies suggests the further thought that in "the shadow of the welfare" the concept of the sheltering tribe is no more; indeed

> Tribal now no longer papa mama
> In relation to the child
> Once your brother's keeper
> Now not even keeper to your child . . .

> Tribal now no longer one for all
> And all for one no longer
> Except in memories of hate
> Umbilical in sulphurous chocolate

Thus, in "the Quarter of the Negroes"—itself a phrase full of anger and irony—tribal togetherness has been replaced by a pervasive hatred of oppressive institutions, mandates, and regulations. This hatred has become the only "umbilical cord" tying one black person to another, but it provides no tribal shelter for the unwed mother, the unwanted child, the unemployed father, or for any of those who "just wait" in the "shadow of the welfare."

In other respects, *Ask Your Mama* is not a typical jazz poem. Certain passages are obscure and recondite and hence lack the direct clarity of statement usually found in the jazz poem. For instance, in the following lines there is the suggestion of a blues cameo in which fantasy is juxtaposed with reality, but the explicit meaning of the lines is somewhat elusive:

> Hip boots
> Deep in the blues

> (And I never had a hip boot on)
> Hair
> Blowing back in the wind
> (And I never had that much hair)
> Diamonds in pawn
> (And I never had a diamond in
> my natural life)
> Me
> In the White House
> (And ain't never had a black house)
> Do, Jesus!
> Lord!
> Amen!

The musical notes accompanying this passage call for a series of gradually fading blues solos by several instruments, "leaving only the flute at the end playing a whimsical little blues of its own." If one consults the "Liner Notes for the Poetically Unhep" at the end of the volume to seek help in construing the specific meaning of these lines, one finds only a very succinct summary of this general section and no specific clarification of the lines in question.

Hughes also complicates his communication problem in *Ask Your Mama* by making excessive use of thematic discontinuity, a rhetorical ploy adapted from the bebop musical style and used with some effectiveness in blending a musical mode with a poetic style in *Montage* in 1951. But in the 1961 volume the message is frequently marred and coherence lost when there are sudden shifts of meaning and thematic breaks that snap the thread of meaning in a given passage and splinter off into elusive tangents of poetical comment which confuse rather than clarify. Such an example is found at the beginning of the second section entitled "Ride Red Ride." After a short passage describing the frustrated search for a woman in the Spanish Quarter of the Negroes ("tu abuela, donde esta?"), the subject shifts suddenly to an ironic comment about Senator Eastland prosecuting Santa Claus for political subversion:

> Santa Claus, forgive me,
> But your gift books are subversive,
> Your dolls are interracial.
> You'll be called by Eastland,
> When they ask you if you knew me,
> Don't take the fifth amendment.

These lines are full of Hughes's own blend of humor and irony, but they have no immediate relationship to the lines immediately preceding.

Another example of this kind of thematic discontinuity occurs at the beginning of the poem when the poet communicates how dismal and isolated and fragile is "the Quarter of the Negroes," whatever the country or climate. The houses have doors of paper and the wind can't wait "for fun to blow doors open." The Quarter is also isolated between river and railroad, but, ironically, the inhabitants of the Quarter have no money for traveling on either railroad or river. Here "boundaries bind" and "no trains or steamboats" travel in any direction. Here life is flat and filled with the gray monotony that afflicts the poor. Yet there is a glittering exception to this state of affairs, and that is found in the life-style of Leontyne:

> Yet Leontyne's unpacking
> In the Quarter of the Negroes
> Where the doorknob lets in lieder
> More than German ever bore,
> Her yesterday past grandpa
> Not of her own doing—
> In a pot of collard greens
> Is gently stewing.

The reference in these lines is to the ironic juxtaposition of two cultures in the life-style of opera star Leontyne Price; she likes to sing German lieder and she likes to eat southern-style collard greens. And as an international celebrity she travels outside the "Quarter of the Negroes."

Having made this interesting observation about the clash of cultures in the lives of international stars like Leontyne Price, Hughes quickly shifts to what one critic calls his most crippling poetic mannerism—a listing of names of those well-to-do, successful blacks who are brought into view when an African diplomat is sent to visit the Quarter by the State Department. Then there follow five lines describing some problems blacks encounter when they move from one Quarter to another—from Harlem to Long Island. This is followed by a rather elusive and puzzling passage about Ralph Ellison and some other black notables setting sail for Ghana and Guinea, Africa's two newly independent nations. Here too there is some name-calling: Ima-Youra (a probable reference to two English-teaching sisters, Ima and Youra Qualls) and "molto bene mellow baby Pearlie Mae" and "Shalom Aleichem Jimmy Baldwin." Then there are two more short passages—one dealing again with Negroes moving into Westchester County and another remarking that newspapers in the Negro ghetto are more concerned with Ornette Cobb, the musician, than with Moscow. It is only at this point that the author returns to the provocative topic of the clash of cultures in the life of an international star like Leontyne Price:

> In the pot behind the
> Paper doors what's cooking?
> What's smelling, Leontyne?
> Lieder, lovely lieder
> And a leaf of collard green,
> Lovely lieder Leontyne.

Admittedly, if the intention of Hughes were to offer only a collage of his flitting impressions of life in the "Quarter of the Negroes" with no conclusive comment or coherent summarization, then skipping rapidly from one theme to another is as poetically fitting as the ingenious musical soloist who weaves an arabesque of sound around a single musical idea. As Jean Wagner points out in his discussion of *Montage*, however, the direct superimposition of the jazz mode on poetry does not always have felicitous results. One infelicitous result is the fragmentation of idea and mood. A somewhat more curious reader, for instance, would like to explore further the social and psychological implications of Leontyne Price's involvement in two conflicting cultures, or one would like to know more about the history behind the search for the black woman in the Negro quarters of Hispanic America. Is she only a symbol of the black woman raped or stolen by powerful masters or savored as one would savor "a little rum with sugar"? Or was she the one who, in fantasy or fact, was seen "fleeing with Lumumba"?

However, despite the lack of thematic continuity and despite the fact that in many places *Ask Your Mama* is reduced to a collage of quick and somewhat elusive impressions, there are occasional passages and images of impressive poetical power. For instance, an important piece of American history is summarized in the following lines:

> On the big screen of the welfare check
> A lynched tomorrow sways. . . .
> With all deliberate speed a
> Lynched tomorrow sways.

Significantly, these lines fetch their poetic power not from the vividness of a concrete impression but from the vatic power of two images—the "big screen of the welfare check" and the fact that America has a "lynched tomorrow" because welfare has been substituted for work "in the Quarter of the Negro." Another passage of similar power is a direct statement summarizing life "in the Quarter of the Negroes." In fact, these five lines more effectively communicate the message of *Ask Your Mama* than the somewhat flippant title of the volume.

> In the quarter of the Negroes
> Where the pendulum is swinging
> To the shadow of the blues,
> Even when you're winning
> There's no way not to lose.

"Ask your Mama" is one of the more telling phrases employed in playing "the dozens"—a game of competitive derogatory name-calling which has deep roots in black folk life. Actually, Hughes uses the question only when responding to naive questions from whites in newly integrated racial situations:

> And they asked me right at Christmas
> If my blackness would it rub off?
> I said, ask your Mama.

However ludicrous the questions by inquisitive whites, what happens in the newly integrated suburbs of Westchester County is of far less importance than what happens in "the Quarter of the Negroes" where "The one coin in the meter/Keeps the gas on" and "Amen is not an ending/But just a punctuation."

Critical reactions to *Ask Your Mama* were varied. Dudley Fitts, writing in the *New York Times Book Review* (Oct. 1961), thought that Hughes's twelve jazz poems were, for many reasons, essentially a "nonliterary" kind of "stunt poetry." He thought that the Harlem poet may have been influenced by Vachel Lindsay's "Congo," although the latter poem lacked Hughes's "fury of indignation and wild comedy." What disturbed Fitts was that poetry which had to be spoken or shouted to musical accompaniment could not really be poetry in the traditional sense. His conclusion was that *Ask Your Mama* is more of "a nightclub turn" to be performed than a series of poems to be read. James Emanuel gives passing notice to the work in his essay on "The Literary Experiments of Langston Hughes" with the comment that the twelve jazz poems constitute a giant "leap in technique" that "outdistanced critical perceptions" and proved that Hughes fully merited the accolade of innovator given him upon his election to the National Institute of Arts and Letters in 1961. There is no evidence that Emanuel in his observation about "outdistanced" critics was referring to any specific critic or critics; but, certainly, Dudley Fitts's conclusion that *Ask Your Mama* was a "night-club turn" indicates that he was baffled, if not "outdistanced," by Hughes's innovative poetic skill.

To Jean Wagner *Ask Your Mama* represents Hughes's attempt "to achieve a huge synthesis" of all the ideas he had propounded and all of the techniques he had used in his poetry since the beginning in the 1920s. Wagner admits that there are passages and lines in the work that baffle even the most intelligent reader, or, to quote this critic, "The perceptible relationship between image and reality tends at times to shrink into total unintelligibility." But Wagner is so impressed by *Ask Your Mama* that, in his opinion, Hughes's occasional "unintelligibility" is so literarily effective that it can be favorably compared with "the obscurity of a Wallace Stevens" (p. 467). Undoubtedly, the association of Hughes with so renowned a contemporary literary figure is an unsullied critical plus for both *Ask Your Mama* and its author. For those who would still doubt his intent and meaning, Wagner adds that there need be no more difficulty with a Hughesian "unintelligible" passage than with a Joycean "unintelligible" passage; in both we have a special kind of literary creativity in which "words summon one another and come together no longer at the bidding of a thought seeking vigorous expression, but on the basis of kindred sonority and structure." A critical defense of this kind clearly indicates that Jean Wagner was by no means "outdistanced" by Hughes's innovative techniques.

But Wagner does more than make critical generalizations in his discussion of *Ask Your Mama*. He analyzes selected lines and passages to probe for image effectiveness and levels of meaning. One example of his critical method is his examination of the implications of the snow image in the "Ode to Dinah" section (p. 471). The passage is as follows:

> In the quarter of the Negroes
> Where to snow now acclimated
> Shadows show up sharper,
> The one coin in the meter
> Keeps the gas on while the TV
> Fails to get Pearl Bailey
> Since it's snowing on the TV

> This last quarter of centennial
> 100 years of emancipation
> Mechanics need repairing
> For Niagara falls is frozen
> As is custom
> As is custom below zero.

In this passage, Wagner correctly indicates that not only does snow symbolize the black man's alienation; but, against the background of a frozen, whitened landscape, blackness casts a sharper shadow. Next, snow symbolizes white power and, by implication, black neglect. In the snowbound winter there is barely enough money to fix the television set and eliminate the "snow" from the picture. Actually, the "mechanics" of society also need "fixing"; since emancipation in 1863 nothing much has "worked" for the black man. As Wagner states (p. 468):

> At this point, the snow symbolism takes another turn: it is said to be snowing on television . . . and this signifies the whites who still prevent the gears of democracy from functioning freely. Still a brief while away from the celebration of the centenary of Emancipation, January 1, 1863, it is high time to repair the defective mechanism.

Then, the snow image shifts to another level of meaning and suggests a frozen Niagara Falls which in turn becomes a monument to that indomitable "General of Freedom," Harriet Tubman. As relentless and as hard-driving as a wintry storm, she led slaves to freedom in the frozen North.

Wagner also notes the strong note of racial optimism in *Ask Your Mama*. The Reverend Martin Luther King, Jr. is depicted fearlessly riding the "unicorn" of racial victory in the South, although on the horn of the unicorn there are both "blood and moonlight." The critic also remarks about Hughes's salute to *Négritude* when, taking the first or second names of three leaders in the movement—Alioune Diop, Aimé Césaire, and Leopold Sedar Senghor—the poet fashions the following line:

> Alioune Aime Sedar sips his Negritude

And finally, Wagner notes how, "for the first time" Hughes's poetry stresses not only the "dream endlessly deferred" but "the dream come true":

Got there! Yes, I made it! . . .

From nobody and nothing to where I am.

With his critical assessment of *Ask Your Mama*, Wagner concludes his extensive critique of Hughes's poetry. Interestingly enough, there is much more rapport between writer and critic at the end of the long essay than at the beginning. Indeed, Wagner, who was initially disenchanted with Hughes's general poetic posture and more than disturbed by his alleged penchant for writing trivia about the trivial, ends his study of the Harlem poet on a very high level of approval and critical sanction. As indicated above, he excuses the "unintelligible" portions of *Ask Your Mama* on the ground that these passages remind one of similar "obscure" passages in the poetry of Wallace Stevens or in the prose of Joyce. And the merging of jazz and poetry, deemed to be of dubious poetic merit in the earlier *Montage of a Dream Deferred*, is now approved as an innovative technique that helps to give thematic unity and cohesiveness to the "12 Moods for Jazz" of *Ask Your Mama*. Indeed, in Wagner's words, *Ask Your Mama* is a "jazz symphony" with repetitive themes that "copiously overlap one section to another, spreading out, disappearing, and surging up anew at intervals."

Inevitably, in the context of this particular phase of his discussion, Wagner compares the symphonic unity of *Ask Your Mama* with what he deems to be the regrettable lack of unity in *Montage of a Dream Deferred*. In the latter work, all one finds, in the French critic's view, is a "great number of separate, relatively disconnected poems." How Wagner arrived at this opinion about the 1951 volume is a mystery wrapped in an enigma, for *Montage* was almost completely devoted to the unifying purpose of delineating the deferred dreams of urban blacks. In fact, the title of the work strongly suggests such a unifying theme. In any event, the question whether *Ask Your Mama* is technically more sophisticated or unified than *Montage* is moot; for, in the final analysis, literary comparisons of this kind are critically counterproductive. In fact, it may be that Wagner's enthusiastic assessment of the later work merely suggests that a critic's understanding of a writer can, through familiarization, broaden and deepen.

Moreover, the changes taking place in the late 1950s may have helped to bring critic into closer communion with poet. Certainly by 1961 and just prior to the publication of *Les Poètes Négres des États-Unis*, the emerging nations of the Third World began to join the community of nations, bringing with them whole clusters of deferred dreams and thus confirming what Hughes had been observing in Harlem for so many years. And it is significant that at the end of his critical discussion of Hughes's poetry, Wagner concludes what Hughes had long known—that Harlem was in fact a microcosm for a nationwide, black macrocosm. He writes:

> for in his work Harlem is symbol as much as reality. When late at night jazz at last falls silent, and one perceives in the nocturnal stillness the heartbreak of the great black city; when standing "on the edge of hell," "remembering the old lies, the old kicks in the back," a greatly provoked Harlem at last gives vent to its rage . . . then there can be no doubt that, beneath the poet's magic wand, Harlem miraculously overflows its boundaries and takes on the dimensions of all Black America.

In this sentence, critic and poet stand together, sharing the same vision, the same hope, and the same despair.

Langston Hughes's final book of poetry, *The Panther and the Lash*, was assembled prior to his unexpected death on May 22, 1967, and published in July of that year. In many respects it is a somber book, devoid of racial comedy or humor. Within its pages there are no black folk characters luxuriating in the warm richness of the black experience; there are no happy blues singers, no Simples and no Madame Alberta K. Johnsons—no poems that celebrate the vibrancy and color of the black life-style. Instead, the emotional tone of the poems reflects the temper of the times. Between the publication of *Ask Your Mama* and *Panther*, America and the world had teetered on the brink of revolutionary racial change. Not only had the Montgomery miracle occurred in the late 1950s to give black America its first organized victory against racial segregation, but sit-in demonstrations had flared throughout the South and extensive riots seared the congested urban black ghettoes of the North. As a consequence, America and the rest of the world became aware both of the plight of black people and the ever increasing menace of widespread racial violence and revolution. The Reverend Martin Luther King, Jr., astride his unicorn, had spread his doctrine of nonviolent social change for all to hear. His message appealed to people everywhere, but the roots of racial hatred ran so deep in America and elsewhere that many racists were never touched by the sunlight of Christian charity. As Hughes had written in 1951, a mistake had been made at Jamestown more than three hundred years before:

> I am the American heartbreak—
> The rock on which Freedom
> Stumped its toe—
> The great mistake
> That Jamestown made
> Long ago.

Also, by the early 1960s, after the long centuries of anger and anguish, a younger generation of blacks began to question whether social, political, and economic integration was a valid goal for black America. They argued that the society to be "integrated" was too flawed—too crisscrossed by errors of omission and commission; in their view, the American mainstream was a spiritual and ethical "nowhere." So they developed a rhetoric of racial confrontation stressing black separatism and power, and their symbol of protest became the snarling black panther. Although this younger generation continued to revere the method and manner of Dr. King, his emphasis on nonviolent social change became more and more suspect. Apparently they were right, for it had become abundantly clear by the middle of the 1960s that all of the prophets of nonviolence would die by violent means.

But the black revolution of the late fifties and early sixties produced more than a new political and social awareness in black America; it resulted in a remarkable resurgence of poetry by and about blacks. Needless to say, older literary revolutionaries like Langston Hughes found this unique literary explosion heartwarming confirmation of all of their toil and labor. Evidence of the poetry explosion was everywhere. First, there appeared in Harlem a black avant-garde publication called *Umbra* which introduced the work of new young poets like Donald Henderson, Calvin Hernton, and Joe Johnstone. Then, in 1962, Rosey Pool published her anthology *Beyond the Blues: New Poems by American Negroes*. This collection introduced a host of new poetical talent—Lance Jeffers, Margaret Danner, Ted Joans, Mari Evans, Julian Bond, Russell Atkins—to name a few. The Pool anthology was quickly followed, in 1963, by Arna Bontemps's *American Negro Poetry* in which older poets like Robert Hayden, Margaret Walker, and Melvin Tolson were featured but which also introduced younger poets like Donald Hayes, Myron O'Higgins, and Conrad Kent Rivers. In the meantime, in further proof that something akin to a revolution in black poetry was taking place in the early 1960s, Gwendolyn Brooks began to write and publish again, after a silence of eleven years, producing *The Bean Eaters* in 1961, *Selected Poems* in 1963, and *In the*

Mecca in 1964. The early 1960s also saw the appearance of LeRoi Jones's *Twenty-Volume Suicide Note* in 1961 and *The Dead Lecturer* in 1964.

Indeed, the times were so propitious for the publication of black poetry that Melvin Tolson rewrote his *Harlem Gallery* which had lain unpublished for twenty years and presented it, amid considerable critical acclaim, to the enthusiastic poetry audience that miraculously began to appear in the 1960s. What impressed Langston Hughes and others about this revolutionary outburst of black poetry is that it was both a poetry of racial protest and one that celebrated the black life-style throughout the black world. In other words, it was the kind of poetry that had long been Hughes's major concern. As Arthur Davis points out in his comments on Hughes in *From the Dark Tower* (1974), all of his poetry—the Harlem poems, the folk poems, the *Négritude* poems—was devoted to the depiction and delineation "of the wrongs, the sorrows, the humor, and the enduring quality" of black people.

Thus, it was inevitable that Langston Hughes would add his voice to the growing chorus of publishing black poets in the mid-1960s and gather eighty-six poems into his last volume of poetry. It was his obvious intention, through this publication, to ride the crest of current events as he had done so many times before. As in *Ask Your Mama, One-Way Ticket, Fine Clothes to the Jew,* and *The Weary Blues,* the poetry in this volume and the authorial attitude reflect the mood and temper of a particular era. Where writers of other periods and cultures recollected past events and tried to divine their meaning, Hughes usually sought to assess the contemporary—to ferret out truths nestled in the context of current events and issues. His title, *The Panther and the Lash*—such a far cry from the black life-style titles given his other poetical volumes—suggests the bitter racial strife which was then shaking America from stem to stern. The "lash" symbolizes overt and covert white hostility to the black man's thrust for civil rights and first-class citizenship; and the "panther," political symbol of America's most militant racial group, symbolizes black anger and black separatism. Significantly enough, the volume is also subtitled "Poems of Our Times," and of the eighty-six, twenty-six had been written and published at an earlier time. "Christ in Alabama" and "Justice," for instance, were first published in *Scottsboro Limited* in 1932. Intended at that time to give an accurate appraisal of the brutal inequities of southern justice, the poems were still, in the 1960s, "poems of the times," suggesting that despite the passing decades, nothing much had changed. Similarly, several poems of racial protest, previously published in *One-Way Ticket, Fields of Wonder,* and *Montage,* acquired a new meaning and significance during the turbulent years of challenge and change in the 1960s. Thus, in his last volume of poetry Hughes earned an accolade bestowable on few of his fellow poets: he emerges as an artist who not only had the gift for trenchant analysis of the present but who, at the same time, could contemplate future vistas and read the wave of the future. In other words, even though he was the poet of rapid insight and fleet impressions, he rarely became so immersed in the particularities of a given moment that he forgot the future's debt to the present and the present's debt to the past.

Undoubtedly, the most effective poems in *Panther* are the new poems like "Junior Addict," the African poems, and poems on such contemporary happenings as the Birmingham church bombing and death on a Vietnam battlefield. All of these provide poetic comment on matters of the immediate moment, but the ideas contained therein have a certain thematic resiliency that will guarantee some relevancy for years to come. Hughes, for instance, had never, in all of his comments on the Harlem scene, directly confronted the drug question in his poetry; but, by the mid-1960s, the man who had so conscientiously searched out the humor and laughter and dignity of the black life-style could no longer overlook the destructive impact of extensive heroin addiction in Harlem. Hence his lament for "The little boy/who sticks a needle in his arm." Interestingly enough, the "sunrise" that was to save Harlem's "Junior Addicts" from death and despair was to be a "sunrise out of Africa":

> Quick, sunrise, come!
> Sunrise out of Africa,
> Quick, come!
> Sunrise, please come!
> Come! Come!

No help could be expected from governmental or social action agencies. Indeed, since it was "easier to get dope/than to get a job," many had come to feel that there was some malevolent plan to flood Harlem and other black urban areas with "junior addicts." So the only source for help to counter the destruction of America's black youth was, in Hughes's view, the "Mother of Continents," Africa. There can be little doubt that "Junior Addict," originally published in the *Liberator* in 1963, is still, almost a half generation later, a valid poetical comment on what regrettably continues to be a major problem in urban and suburban America.

The six poems on Africa in *Panther* bear the broad title "African Question Mark." There are two kinds of poems in this group—three short poems full of generalized metaphorical comment on abstractions like race and freedom and hope and three longer poems reflecting the poet's direct confrontation with a specific racial event. The appropriateness of the juxtaposition of these two kinds of poems—poems of concrete statement and poems of abstract comment—has been observed above. All of the short poems were written earlier; "History" was published in 1934 in *Opportunity*, "Oppression" in 1947 in *Fields of Wonder*, and "Color" in 1943 in *Jim Crow's Last Stand*. All three poems are reflective and inspirational in tone and seek to inculcate proper attitudes toward socially beneficial abstractions like freedom, color, justice, and racial equity. The other three poems reveal the other side of Hughes as a poet, for these are poems of direct comment on selected current events. Hence, their concern is with the particular, the concrete, and the contemporary. In both kinds of poems there is racial and social protest, but in the earlier short poems, the poet exhorts; in the three longer poems he excoriates. "Lumumba's Grave," for instance, is filled with a terse anger, reminiscent of the anger in the poem "Scottsboro" which Hughes wrote in 1931. In essence, the longer poems reveal Hughes at his impressionistic best, producing an impromptu art wrought out of the anger of the moment. Indeed, the first three stanzas of "Lumumba's Grave" read like a choral dirge laced with racial bitterness:

> Lumumba was black
> And he didn't trust
> The whores all powdered
> With uranium dust.
>
> Lumumba was black
> And he didn't believe
> The lies thieves shook
> Through their "freedom" sieve.
>
> Lumumba was black
> His blood was red—
> And for being a man
> They killed him dead.

There is no rhetorical elaboration here; the lines have the stark clarity and emotional succinctness of a nursery rhyme, but the anger of a poet who loved justice and hated oppression floods the entire poem. The same kind of bitterness, stated with monosyllabic simplicity, is found in the opening lines of "Angola Question Mark," a poem in which the poet speaks through the mouth of a colonized African:

> Don't know why I,
> Black,
> Must still stand
> With my back
> To the last frontier
> Of fear
> In my own land.

Another poem in the volume reflecting an immediate, angry reaction to a gruesome racial incident is "Birmingham Sunday." Here again, the poet directly confronts an event that left most Americans silent and inarticulate in grief and disappointment. Evidently Hughes viewed himself in situations of this kind, as the spokesman-poet who was never permitted the luxury of emotional or esthetic distance from the consequences of man's inhumane behavior toward his fellowman. So, disciplined by his years of experience as a confrontation poet, he wrote as follows of the bombing of four little black children in a black church on a fateful Sunday morning:

> Four little girls
> Who went to Sunday School that day
> And never came back home at all
> But left instead
> Their blood upon the wall
> With spattered flesh
> And bloodied summer dresses
> Torn to shreds by dynamite
> That China made aeons ago—

Such a poem has a dramatic vigor and compressed emotion rarely found in the shorter poems on "Justice" and "Oppression." Yet the details of the poem underscore both the absence of justice and the presence of oppression. Poems like "Birmingham Sunday" underscore Hughes's ability to make a vigorous poetical pronouncement about those awesome and crushing events that leave ordinary people groping around in stunned silence. This ability makes him more than a "social poet"—a sobriquet used in *Phylon* in 1948 when he sought to describe his role and function as a poet. Actually, "Bir-

mingham Sunday" and "Lumumba's Grave" are poems of emotional confrontation. They lack the blatant rhetorical violence of
the confrontation poetry of the late 1960s, but they contain a strong
man's forthright response to man's inhumanity to man.

As has been indicated above, *The Panther and the Lash* was, in
mood and tone, a far cry from *Ask Your Mama*, published a short
six years before. The flippant insouciance, the experimental flair,
the jazz overtones and undertones are all absent. This is understandable; in the 1960s the absurdities and ironies of integration no longer
commanded poetic attention, and the violence of a blood-spattered
decade made humor and laughter obsolete. So Hughes adapted to
the times, just as he had in the mid-1920s when jazz and blues were
king, in the 1930s when social unrest and economic depression domi-
nated the scene, or in the mid-1950s when bebop was a new and
exciting creative style.

Probably because *Panther* was published posthumously in racially
turbulent times, the volume attracted relatively scant published
critical response. Keneth Kinnamon, in a collective assessment of
the work of "The Man Who Created Simple" in the *Nation* (Dec.
1967) includes a somewhat modified review of *Panther*; and later,
Laurence Lieberman, in his 1968 review of the recent work of six
contemporary poets, includes Hughes's last volume among the
works noted. Kinnamon, guided by a ranked list of Hughes's "best"
poetry taken from James Emanuel's *Langston Hughes*, concludes
that Hughes's best poems were written and published in the 1920s.
It is also his conclusion that, although there were "developments"
during Hughes's long poetical career, there was no discernible
"artistic growth"—an interpretation quite at variance with the conclusions reached by Wagner and later by Emanuel concerning
innovation and change in Hughes's poetic technique during the
1950s and 1960s. The inference to be drawn from Kinnamon's endorsement of Emanuel's ranking of Hughes's "best" poems is that
Panther, which contains none of these "best" poems published in the
1920s and only two poems published in the 1930s, is not an exceptional performance.

Kinnamon was also disenchanted with the poet's apparent stress
on the value of racial integration as a desirable social and political
goal for black Americans in the late 1960s. Hughes's "inability to
relinquish the dream of racial fraternity even in the Deep South"
made him, in Kinnamon's view, something of an anachronism in a
period in which integrationism was "all but dead among Negro
writers." Kinnamon also stresses that only those poems of racial
protest which "catch the threatening mood of impending black

retributive vengeance" and champion black separatism were in tune
with the times; those depicting "the Negro as passive victim" or
pro-integrationist no longer had relevance. Unfortunately, this
critic's review format (actually a somewhat compressed assessment
of *Panther*, Hughes's edition of *Best Short Stories by Negroes*,
Emanuel's *Langston Hughes*, and Dickinson's *Bio-Bibliography* all
rolled into one) afforded little space for additional specific comment
and definition of these two kinds of protest poetry, particularly as
seen in *Panther*. Nor did he have an opportunity to indicate why
those "recent poems" which did "catch the . . . mood of impending
black retributive vengeance" were not included by Emanuel among
Hughes's best or why he (Kinnamon) classified only the "early
poetry" as "a lasting achievement" in American black literature.
Some substantive analysis of both early and late poems in *Panther*
might have helped to resolve this apparent contradiction.

In Kinnamon's defense it should be stated that he was probably
misled by some of the critical conclusions reached by Emanuel in
Langston Hughes: Black Genius (1967). This critical biography
exudes a tone of almost breathless rapidity, as if the time and space
needed to cover all of the parts of Hughes's many-faceted career
were in critically short supply. So critical observations are compressed, chronology telescoped, and explications condensed and
attenuated. For instance, observations about the critical reception of
Shakespeare in Harlem are highly generalized and nonspecific:

> The press called *Shakespeare in Harlem* melancholy, biting,
> and grim despite its hilarity and the author's prefatory descrip-
> tion of it as "light verse;" reviewers saw it as conscious artistry
> in control of a refined social sensitivity.

The comments on the reaction to *Fields of Wonder* are similar:

> Of *Fields of Wonder*, reviewers generally implied that the
> many poems reflecting the author's nonracial experience lacked
> the ardor and the "oceanic turbulence" . . . of his earlier poetry.

Sometimes these generalized observations are of puzzling import:

> . . . *One-Way Ticket* fared the worst in the press. Some com-
> mentators almost wistfully recorded their preference for his
> earlier works while mildly emphasizing the forbearance, hu-
> mor, and directness in the poems in the new book. Others la-
> beled the volume "thin and artificial" or they mixed old praise

with new blame by observing that his present "jejune and iterative" verse left his reputation still undimmed.

Fortunately, Emanuel does occasionally vary this format and provide his own somewhat abbreviated critical comment on the blues, jazz, and *Négritude* poems. For instance, after two or three pages of sustained critical discussion of *Ask Your Mama*, it is his conclusion that it is "an oddly balanced work of old and new tensions"—a work over which hovers "A certain fluidity of time and illusiveness of place." Basically, however, there is a lack of sustained and informed poetical criticism in Emanuel's study: for example, he mentions Wagner's *Les Poètes Négres des États-Unis* only once and that is in his bibliography and not in his text, even though that book was available as early as 1963.

For these reasons, it is more than odd that in a work containing little or no rigorous criticism either of Hughes's poetry or of the poet's critics, the writer should suddenly conclude his study with an authoritarian listing of the poet's ten best poems, "ranked in their apparent order of excellence." It is in every sense an ex cathedra pronouncement, delivered without any supporting evidence or documentation. Of the hundreds of poems written by Hughes over a forty-five-year period, Emanuel says, without the quiver of a critical eyelash:

> the following ten, ranked in their apparent order of excellence, are his best: "Mulatto," "The Negro Speaks of Rivers," "Song for a Dark Girl," "Jazzonia," "The Negro Mother," "Dream Variations," "The Breath of a Rose," "Minstrel Man," "Evenin Air Blues," and "Dream Boogie."

As Kinnamon notes, all of these, "Dream Boogie" excepted, are products of Hughes's early years, a fact undoubtedly indicative of a yet unexplained bias of Emanuel in favor of the early poetry. Interestingly enough, possibly because of this fairly pronounced bias, Emanuel makes only one reference to Hughes's last volume of poetry, dismissing *Panther* as a collection of poems that "reflect the racially turbulent years climaxed by the Black Panther Party and the 'white backlash.'" Like many observations in Emanuel's book, this comment is void of critical substance.

Laurence Lieberman's review of *Panther* begins with a different set of assumptions from those held by Kinnamon and thus arrives at a different set of conclusions. Lieberman makes no mention of the "zero growth" assumption about Hughes's artistic development as a poet nor any mention of Emanuel's ranked listing of Hughes's "best" poetry. In fact, where Kinnamon praises the early poetry and by implication devaluates the later poetry, Lieberman indicates that some of the new poems in *Panther* were the best of a long and productive career. He writes:

> To a degree I would never have expected from his earlier work, his sensibility has kept pace with the times, and the intensity of his new concerns . . . comes to fruition in many of the best poems of his career: "Northern Liberal," "Dinner Guest: Me," "Crowns and Garlands," to name a few.

Lieberman also praises the early poem "Justice" as an example of Hughes's "knack of investing metaphor with a fierce potency." The depiction of justice as a blind goddess with "festering sores" for eyes is, in his opinion, both politically and poetically stimulating. But Lieberman does have three negative comments about the poems in Hughes's last volume. First, he finds it unfortunate that "in different poems" Hughes assumed "starkly antithetical" political positions. Some poems reveal an aggressive black powerism, others a more moderate integrationism. Lieberman's concern that Hughes discard the mask of racial or political neutralism and adopt a more aggressive racial stance was, in 1968, an understandable concern. Not that the critic did not think the poet's "catholicity" of political views praiseworthy and his "tolerance of all the rival . . . views of his . . . compatriots" commendable. But Lieberman asks, where did Hughes himself stand? What were his racial politics? For, says the critic, "A poetry whose chief claim on our attention is moral, rather than aesthetic, must take sides politically." Because he cannot find a well-defined political position in *Panther*, his conclusion is that Hughes, in a poem like "Black Panther," was "less concerned with approving or disapproving of Black Power than with demonstrating the necessity and inevitability of the shift" in racial politics during the 1960s. Lieberman could have added that in other times and in other climes there were poets who sought to develop a "wise disinterestedness" on political issues and yet remain concerned advocates of truth, justice, and equity.

Lieberman's second negative criticism is of Hughes's "ungovernable weakness for essayistic polemicizing that distracts the poet from the more serious demands of his art." Here Lieberman strikes at the heart of the problem confronting a poet whose concern was with the current and the contemporary. Inevitably, some "essayistic polemicizing" crept into Hughes's poetry, thus on occasion substituting preachments for poetics. And it might be added that all or most writers of protest poetry run this risk.

Lieberman's third complaint is against Hughes's practice of "heroic cataloguing" or listing names of important persons in some of his poems. Lieberman would excuse such cataloguing under some circumstances, but when it becomes "the structural mainstay" of a poem, then "self-conscious historicity" displaces genuine poetry. As indicated above, this practice did rob several passages of *Ask Your Mama* of poetical power.

Two additional critical reviews of *Panther* warrant mention here. Both were published in the *CLA Journal*, a scholarly periodical that devoted its entire final issue of June 1968 to essays on the literary career of Langston Hughes. The first review, written by W. E. Farrison, appeared in the March 1968 issue. It is a comprehensive and clearly stated evaluation of Hughes's final volume of verse, reflecting the solid competence usually found in the work of this literary scholar deemed by many to be "the dean of Afro-American literary studies." Farrison sees in the eighty-six poems of *Panther* the usual Hughesian blend of irony, satire, and militant protest. In his view, "Black Panther" is a militant poem reminiscent of McKay's "If We Must Die," and he notes the bitter irony in the section entitled "American Heartbreak." And, unlike Kinnamon, Farrison sees in the "Daybreak in Alabama" section a confirmation of Hughes's optimistic faith in American democracy and not evidence of a less-than-honorable integrationist compromise. He also finds the poems in the section "Face of War" to be "especially noteworthy," particularly the poem "Without Benefit of Declaration." For some reason, neither Kinnamon nor Lieberman reacted to this section in which Hughes, in something of a fine prophetic frenzy, confronted the personal heartbreak of the Viet Nam War which was to become by the early 1970s a heavy albatross around America's neck. Also, in the course of his discussion Farrison identifies, with typical scholarly zeal, "Backlash Blues" as the last poem which Hughes submitted to the publisher before his death. He also demonstrates how earlier poems in *One-Way Ticket* accurately forecast the events of the 1960s. Farrison's conclusion is that *Panther* is a "vital contribution" to the Negro's struggle "as well as to American poetry."

Theodore Hudson's brief essay "Langston Hughes' Last Volume of Verse" (*CLA Journal*, June 1968) is a far less positive assessment than those provided by either Farrison, Kinnamon, or Lieberman. Hudson begins by expressing his longtime admiration for Hughes's philosophy and general literary demeanor. He likes the fact that

Hughes was militant in his poetry but "incapable of acrimony." "Empathy," not "hate," was the Hughesian "bag," and everything was coated with his "whimsical, ironical, and gently satirical humor." But the poems in *Panther* are not typical of the Hughes Hudson had so long admired. They are full of the kind of "flat and direct statement" which produced lines of poetry "that plod rather than soar." The poems of *Panther* consequently contain more of the "prosaic" than of the "poetic." They "stimulate the mind" but "often do not reverberate in one's heart." Because they are so "grimly earnest" in their protest, the poet "declaims" too much and "sings" too little. Unfortunately, Hudson provides no documented support of these neatly balanced but somewhat pejorative critical generalizations. Accordingly, all that can be said is that his review reflects a kind of romantic or nostalgic longing for the poetry of an earlier Hughes, when the poems had more "spontaneity" and "a natural lilt" in language and idiom. Thus, Hudson's critical position in a sense reflects that of both Kinnamon and Emanuel, namely, that Hughes's early poems are generally better than his later ones. Such a conclusion, of course, needs critical substantiation—something missing from the critical assessments of all three of these writers. It is hoped that future critical studies of Hughes's poetry will address this issue and examine the ranges of creativity which are assumed to be inevitable in a long and productive literary career.

The publication of *Panther* marked the end of Langston Hughes's sturdy and enduring trek up the Parnassus of poetical achievement. Throughout his almost fifty years of continued publication, many critics responded and reacted to what he had written. What these critics wrote is an important part of the Langston Hughes story. Their critical observations will help future generations gain a deeper understanding of trends and developments in black poetry between 1920 and 1970.

References

Baldwin, James
    1955. *Notes of a Native Son*. Boston: Beacon.
    1959. "Review of *Selected Poems*," *New York Times Book Review* March 29, p. 6.
Bontemps, Arna
    1963. (editor) *American Negro Poetry*. New York: Hill & Wang.
Brooks, Gwendolyn
    1975. *Part One*. Detroit: Broadside Pr.
Brown, Lloyd L.
    1959. (letter) *New York Times Book Review* May 24, p. 42.

Cardone-Hine, Alvero
1959. "Review of *Selected Poems*," *Mainstream* July, pp. 55–56.
Cullen, Countee
1947. *On These I Stand*. New York: Harper.
Davis, Arthur
1974. *From the Dark Tower*. Washington, D.C.: Howard Univ. Pr.
Eliot, T. S.
1943. *Four Quartets*. New York: Harcourt.
Emanuel, James
1967. *Langston Hughes*. New York: Twayne.
1971. "The Literary Experiments of Langston Hughes." In *Langston Hughes: Black Genius*, edited by Therman O'Daniel, pp. 171–82. New York: Morrow.
Farrison, W. Edward
1968. "Review of *Panther and the Lash*," *CLA Journal* Mar., pp. 259–61.
Fitts, Dudley
1961. "Review of *Ask Your Mama*," *New York Times Book Review* Oct. 29, p. 16.
Hudson, Theodore
1968. "Langston Hughes' Last Volume of Verse," *CLA Journal* June, pp. 345–48.
Hughes, Langston
1956. "From Harlem to Paris," *New York Times Book Review* Feb. 26, p. 3.
Kinnamon, Keneth
1967. "The Man Who Created Simple," *Nation* Dec., pp. 599–601.
Lieberman, Laurence
1968. "Poetry Chronicle," *Poetry* Aug., pp. 337–43.
Parker, John W.
1959. "Review of *Selected Poems*," *Phylon* Summer, pp. 196–97.
Rexroth, Kenneth
1958. "Jazz Poetry," *Nation* Mar. 29, p. 282.
Wagner, Jean
1962. *Les Poètes Négres des États-Unis*. Paris: Librairie Ista.
Walker, Margaret
1950. "New Poets," *Phylon* 11:345–54.
Winslow, Henry
1959. "Review of *Selected Poems*," *Crisis* Oct., pp. 512–13.

CHAPTER 6

Questions in Search of Answers

When Langston Hughes died in 1967, there were many tributes to this writer who for fifty years had occupied a central place on the black American literary scene. Published tributes of praise were to be found in every major literary journal, and learned panegyrists competed with each other to celebrate the contributions and achievements of this very versatile writer. Some journals—*Présence Africaine, Negro Digest, CLA Journal*—even devoted whole issues to memorializing this distinguished man of letters. By 1970, however, all farewells had been made, and scholars were free to start a reassessment of Hughes which is still underway.

Inevitably, his death left many questions hanging. One which has been asked repeatedly: was Hughes really as good a writer as certain anthology editors somewhat defensively asserted when, in the 1940s and 1950s, they sought to integrate their literary collections by slipping in one or two of his poems or short stories? Also, when Hughes called himself "the dream-keeper," was his misnomer intentional or had he really beguiled himself into believing that he was the spinner of silken dreams in the nightmarish world of urban poverty and crime. And there are other questions. Did he spread himself too thinly over too many genres? Did he concentrate too much on Harlem, or America's race problems, or on the world's race problems? Was he lacking in a requisite high seriousness on occasion and too often given to flippancy and the glib retort? Was, as several critics have asserted, his best time his early period and the remaining thirty years—from the 1930s on—an agonizingly prolonged downhill literary glide? And what of the irony of a black poet who stood almost alone for so many years and then, as death beckoned in the late 1960s, found himself suddenly surrounded by a teeming host of new black poets? Were these new poets really indebted to him? Although of a different breed, style, and manner, did they—Sonia Sanchez, Don Lee, Ethridge Knight—bask in the older poet's afterglow? Like jungle orchids, they had sprung forth from the rubble of riot-torn cities—cities which the older poet had predicted would one day explode. At least Hughes had asked and answered the definitive question: "What happens to a dream deferred?/Does it explode?" But the older poet had asked that question way back in 1951 at a time when no one believed that the combustibility of a cluster of deferred dreams was any more than a weak poetic image fashioned by an author whose effective poetic power, according to some, had almost completely disappeared twenty years earlier.

Two facts are obvious. First, few of these questions are fully answerable at this time. Second, it is easy to understand how the long career of a writer as prolific as Hughes would provoke so many questions. By far the most provocative question of all is whether Hughes as poet reached his acme of development in the 1920s and thereafter sank down to a low plateau of poetic accomplishment. Several critics—Calverton, Cruse, Kinnamon, Emanuel, and Hudson, for example—have so stated. It is interesting to note that in making such a critical judgment they have, unwittingly or not, thrust Hughes into the middle of a distinguished company. William Wordsworth, for instance, went into some kind of poetic decline after 1807 that lasted until his death forty-three years later. At least this is the interpretation of a substantial body of Wordsworthian critics. The fact that this Romantic poet was named poet laureate in 1842—at the height of his decline, as it were—only leads these critics to make scabrous comments about the dismal state of the laureateship during the 1840s, thanks to very minor laureates like Bob Southey and his kind. But there have been other long-lived poets besides Wordsworth who, after auspicious beginnings, never "recaptured that first fine careless rapture." The careers of both Eliot and Pound come to mind. A possible explanation of this phenomenon is that the ability to be intensively creative is necessarily of brief duration. Hence, poets who die young are usually good poets, and few poets can sustain a high level of creativity for more than a few bright years. Poets who, like Wordsworth and Hughes, continue to live on and write and publish have little to say after that first fine outburst.

Needless to say, some literary skeptics will have no part of any such critical theory. If applied to Hughes, it does raise some additional questions. For instance, one might venture to ask whether Hughes's involvement with leftist causes and leftist poetry precipitated his poetic decline in the 1930s. Did he veer from poetry to propaganda and thus wreak his poetic undoing? Or did Hughes as writer take on a special ambience in the 1920s because of his masterful and impassioned defense of the cause of black folk poetry against the opinions of an entrenched and conservative black, upper middle class? This aspect of Hughes's career could conceivably have had a strong influence on some critics. Unfortunately, during the remainder of his career there were no more such acts of youthful challenge, simply because, as one grows older, there are fewer opportunities for youthful behavior of any kind. In the 1930s and 1940s Hughes had continuing confrontations with Aimee Semple McPherson, with the religious establishment, with the white South, and, ultimately, with the federal government; but none of these had the sparkle and intensity of the poet's attack on the literary and cultural standards of black critics of the "talented tenth" persuasion. Finally, what of the quality of later volumes—*One-Way Ticket, Montage, Ask Your Mama, Panther?* Was Hughes's performance in these works demonstrably worse than anything that he published in the 1920s?

Answers to questions of this kind can be provided only after intensive study of the dynamic interaction between Hughes's patterns of creativity and the social, cultural, and political climate in which specific poems or groups of poems were written. For he was a poet who immersed himself in the contemporary and the current and often wrote poems to explicate political, social, and emotional reactions. Indeed, to some critics this poetical characteristic was one of Hughes's major limitations as a poet: intensely involved in the flotsam and jetsam of contemporary incident, he was much too issue-oriented and his work often lacked universality.

Fortunately, Jean Wagner, who has given Hughes's poetry its most thorough analysis to date, employs a thematic, and not a chronological, approach in his criticism. Therefore, the French critic is not hampered by extraneous concerns and is free to explicate the poems on the basis of actual content and not on the basis of assumed intent. His conclusion is that Hughes's poetry, from 1921 to 1927, reveals no decline in quality after *Fine Clothes to the Jew* (1927). Rather, there are good lines and sound poetic concepts in all of the books of poetry right down through *Panther* in 1967. This is not to say that Wagner, like Alain Locke, was not appalled by Hughes's regrettable penchant for mingling "dishwater" lines with "crystal-spring" images.

In the final analysis, the comparative value of Hughes's poetry at any given time or period can only be determined after the conscientious critical examination all good poets merit but few of them get. We need to know with some specificity why and how a Hughesian dramatic monologue of the 1920s like "Mother to Son" is better or worse than "Ballad of the Landlord" which was written in 1940. In such an examination, unsubstantiated generalizations must be avoided and all critical conclusions carefully supported by relevant evidence. In the meantime, while we await such a definitive critical study, we can enjoy the work of this poet who, from 1921 until his death in 1967, wrote and published thousands of poems— some good, some bad, and some of indifferent quality. During these years, this poet heard the tom-tom laugh and he heard the tom-tom cry; and when, using the simple accents of the folk, he related what he had heard, the black world stopped to listen, to learn, and to laugh. All racial wounds were not instantly healed, but the world well knew that a gifted black folk poet had passed this way.

Bibliography

Works by Langston Hughes

POETRY
(in order of publication)

The Weary Blues. New York: Knopf, 1926.
Fine Clothes to the Jew. New York: Knopf, 1927.
Dear Lovely Death. Amenia, New York: Troutbeck Pr., 1931.
The Negro Mother. New York: Golden Stair Pr., 1931.
The Dream-Keeper and Other Poems. New York: Knopf, 1932.
Scottsboro Limited. New York: Golden Stair Pr., 1932.
A New Song. New York: International Workers Order, 1938.
Shakespeare in Harlem. New York: Knopf, 1942.
Freedom's Plow. New York: Musette Publishing, 1943.
Jim Crow's Last Stand. Atlanta: Negro Publishing, 1943.
Fields of Wonder. New York: Knopf, 1947.
One-Way Ticket. New York: Knopf, 1949.
Montage of a Dream Deferred. New York: Henry Holt, 1951.
Selected Poems. New York: Knopf, 1959.
Ask Your Mama. New York: Knopf, 1961.
The Panther and the Lash. New York: Knopf, 1967.

NOVELS
(in order of publication)

Not Without Laughter. New York: Knopf, 1930.
Simple Speaks his Mind. New York: Simon and Schuster, 1950.
Simple Takes a Wife. New York: Simon and Schuster, 1953.
Simple Stakes a Claim. New York: Rinehart, 1957.
Tambourines to Glory. New York: Day, 1958.
The Best of Simple. New York: Hill & Wang, 1961.
Simple's Uncle Sam. New York: Hill & Wang, 1965.

SHORT STORIES
(in order of publication)

The Ways of White Folks. New York: Knopf, 1934.

Laughing to Keep from Crying. New York: Henry Holt, 1952.
Something in Common and Other Stories. New York: Hill & Wang, 1963.

DRAMA
(in order of presentation)

Mulatto. A three-act tragedy. Produced at the Vanderbilt Theatre on Broadway, New York City, 1935. First published in English in *Five Plays by Langston Hughes*, edited by Webster Smalley. Bloomington: Indiana Univ. Pr., 1963, pp. 1–25.

Little Ham. A three-act comedy. Produced by the Gilpin Players of Cleveland, Ohio, 1935. In *Five Plays by Langston Hughes*, pp. 43–112.

Troubled Island. A three-act tragedy. Produced by the Gilpin Players, 1935-36.

When the Jack Hollers. A three-act comedy. By Langston Hughes in collaboration with Arna Bontemps. Produced by the Gilpin Players, 1936.

Joy to my Soul. A three-act comedy. Produced by the Gilpin Players, 1937.

Soul Gone Home. A one-act fantasy. Produced by the Cleveland Federal Theatre, Cleveland, Ohio, 1937. Published in *One Act Play Magazine* (July 1937). Also in *Five Plays by Langston Hughes*, pp. 37–42.

Don't You Want to be Free? A long one-act play. Produced by Negro amateur groups in major American cities, 1937. Set a performance record (135 performances) at the New York Suitcase Theatre, New York City, 1938. Published in *One Act Play Magazine* (Oct. 1938), 359–93.

Front Porch. Three-act comedy-drama. Produced by the Gilpin Players, 1938.

The Sun Do Move. A musical drama. Produced by the Skyloft Players, Chicago, Illinois, 1942.

Simply Heavenly. A two-act comedy. Presented at Eighty-fifth Street Playhouse, New York City, 1957. Published in *Five Plays by Langston Hughes*, pp. 113–81 and in *The Langston Hughes Reader*, pp. 244–313.

Tambourines to Glory. A two-act gospel singing play adapted from the novel of the same name. Presented at The Little Theatre, New York City, 1963. In *Five Plays by Langston Hughes*, pp. 182–258.

TRANSLATIONS
(in order of publication)

Roumain, Jacques. *Masters of the Dew* [*Gouverneurs de la Rosée*]. Translated with Mercer Cook. New York: Reynal and Hitchcock, 1947.

Guillén, Nicolás. *Cuba Libre.* Translated with Ben Carruthers. Los Angeles: The Ward Ritchie Pr., 1948.

Garcia Lorca, Federico. *Gypsy Ballads. Beloit Poetry Chapbook,* No. 1. Beloit, Wis.: Beloit College, 1951.

Selected Poems of Gabriela Mistral [Lucila Godoy Alcayaga]. Bloomington: Indiana Univ. Pr., 1957.

Diop, David. "Those Who Lost Everything" and "Suffer, Poor Negro." In *Poems from Black Africa, Ethiopia, and Other Countries,* edited by Langston Hughes, pp. 143–45. Bloomington: Indiana Univ. Pr., 1963.

Rabearivelo, Jean-Joseph. "Flute Players." In *Poems from Black Africa,* pp. 131–32.

Roumain, Jacques. "When the Tom-Tom Beats" and "Guinea." In *Anthology of Contemporary Latin-American Poetry,* edited by Dudley Fitts, pp. 191, 193. Norfolk, Conn.: New Directions, 1942.

Pedroso, Regino. "Opinions of the New Chinese Student." In *Anthology of Contemporary Latin-American Poetry,* pp. 247, 249.

Damas, Leon. "Really I Know," "Trite Without Doubt," and "She Left Herself One Evening." In *The Poetry of the Negro, 1746–1949,* pp. 371–372.

AUTOBIOGRAPHIES
(in order of publication)

The Big Sea: An Autobiography. New York: Knopf, 1940.

I Wonder as I Wander: An Autobiographical Journey. New York: Rinehart, 1956.

HISTORY AND BIOGRAPHY
(in order of publication)

The First Book of Negroes. New York: Watts, 1951.

The First Book of Rhythms. New York: Watts, 1954.

Famous American Negroes. New York: Dodd, Mead, 1954.

Famous Negro Music-Makers. New York: Dodd, Mead, 1955.

The First Book of Jazz. New York: Watts, 1955.

The First Book of the West Indies. New York: Watts, 1956.

A Pictorial History of the Negro in America. With Milton Meltzer. New York: Crown, 1956.

Famous Negro Heroes of America. New York: Dodd, Mead, 1958.

First Book of Africa. New York: Watts, 1960.

Fight for Freedom: The Story of the NAACP. New York: Norton, 1962.

Black Magic: A Pictorial History of the Negro in American Entertainment. With Milton Meltzer. New Jersey: Prentice-Hall, 1967.

EDITED ANTHOLOGIES
(in order of publication)

Four Lincoln University Poets. Chester, Pa.: Lincoln Univ., 1930.

The Poetry of the Negro, 1746-1949. With Arna Bontemps. Garden City: Doubleday, 1949.

The Book of Negro Folklore. With Arna Bontemps. New York: Dodd, Mead, 1959.

An African Treasury: Articles, Essays, Stories, Poems by Black Africans. New York: Crown, 1960.

Poems from Black Africa, Ethiopia, and Other Countries. Bloomington: Indiana Univ. Pr., 1963.

New Negro Poets: U.S.A. Bloomington: Indiana Univ. Pr., 1964.

The Book of Negro Humor. New York: Dodd, Mead, 1966.

The Best Short Stories by Negro Writers: An Anthology from 1899 to the Present. Boston: Little, 1967.

Additional Selected Materials

Allen, Samuel W. "Negritude and its Relevance to the American Negro Writer." *The American Negro Writer and His Roots.* New York: American Society of African Culture, 1960, pp. 8–20.

Allen, William. "The Barrier: A Critique." *Phylon* 11:134–36.

Bardolph, Richard. *The Negro Vanguard.* New York: Rinehart, 1959.

Barksdale, Richard K. "White Triangles, Black Circles." *CLA Journal* 18:465–76.

Berry, Faith, ed. *Good Morning Revolution.* New York: Lawrence Hill, 1973.

———. Voice for the Jazz Age, Great Migration or Black Bourgeoisie." *Black World* 20:10–16.

Blassingame, John W. "Black Autobiographies as History and Literature." *Black Scholar* 4:2–9.

Bone, Robert A. *The Negro Novel in America.* New Haven: Yale Univ. Pr., 1958.

Bontemps, Arna. "The Black Renaissance of the Twenties." *Black World* 20:5–9.

———. "The Two Harlems." *American Scholar* 14:167–73.

———. "The Harlem Renaissance." *Saturday Review of Literature* 30:12–13, 44.

———. "Negro Poets, Then and Now." *Phylon* 11:355–60.

———. "Langston Hughes: He Spoke of Rivers." *Freedomways* 8:140–43.

Brawley, Benjamin. *The Negro Genius.* New York: Dodd, Mead, 1937.

———. "The Negro Literary Renaissance." *Southern Workman* 56:177–80.

Brooks, A. Russell. "The Comic Spirit and the Negro's New Look." *CLA Journal* 6:35–43.

Brown, Lloyd W. "Black Entitles: Names as Symbols in Afro-American Literature." *Studies in Black Literature* 1:16–44.

———. "The Portrait of the Artist as a Black American in the Poetry of Langston Hughes." *Studies in Black Literature* 5:24–27.

Brown, Sterling A. "Not Without Laughter." *Opportunity* 8:279–80.

———. *The Negro in American Fiction*. Bronze Booklet No. 6. Washington: Associates in Negro Folk Education, 1937.

———. *Negro Poetry and Drama*. Bronze Booklet No. 7. Washington: Associates in Negro Folk Education, 1937.

Budd, Louis J. "The Not So Tender Traps: Some Dilemmas of Black American Poets." *Indian Journal of American Studies* 3:47–57.

Calverton, V. F. "This Negro." *Nation* 131:157–58.

———. *The Liberation of American Literature*. New York: Scribner, 1932.

———. "The Negro and American Culture." *Saturday Review of Literature* 22:3–4, 17–18.

Cargill, Oscar. *Intellectual America: Ideas on the March*. New York: Macmillan, 1941.

Carmen, Y. "Langston Hughes: Poet of the People." *International Literature* 1:192–94.

Carrington, Glenn. "The Harlem Renaissance—A Personal Memoir." *Freedomways* 3:307–11.

Cartey, Wilfred. "Four Shadows of Harlem." *Negro Digest* 18:22–25, 83–92.

Chamberlain, John. "The Negro as Writer." *Bookman* 70:603–11.

Chapman, Abraham. "The Harlem Renaissance in Literary History." *CLA Journal* 11:38–58.

Clarke, John Henrik. "The Neglected Dimensions of the Harlem Renaissance." *Black World* 20:118–29.

———. "Langston Hughes and Jesse B. Semple." *Freedomways* 8:167–69.

Cobb, Martha K. "Concepts of Blackness in the Poetry of Nicholas Guillen, Jacques Roumain and Langston Hughes." *CLA Journal* 18:262–72.

Collier, Eugenia W. "Heritage from Harlem." *Black World* 20:52–59.

Combecher, Hans. "Zu einem Gedicht von Langston Hughes: 'Minstrel Man.' " *Die Neueren Sprachen* 15:184–287.

———. "Interpretationen für den Englischunterricht: Langston Hughes, F. R. Scott, T. S. Eliot." *Neueren Sprachen* 17:506–14.

Cook, Mercer, and Henderson, Stephen E. *The Militant Black Writer in Africa and the United States*. Madison: Univ. of Wisconsin Pr., 1969.

Dance, Daryl C. "Contemporary Militant Black Humor." *Negro American Literary Forum* 8:217–22.

Dandridge, Rita B. "The Black Woman as Freedom Fighter in Langston Hughes' *Simple's Uncle Sam.*" *CLA Journal* 18:273–83.

Davis, Allison. "Our Negro Intellectuals." *Crisis* 35:268–69.

Davis, Arthur. *From the Dark Tower: Afro-American Writers from 1900-1960.* Washington, D.C.: Howard Univ. Pr., 1974.

———. "The Harlem of Langston Hughes' Poetry." *Phylon* 8:276–83.

———. "Jesse B. Semple: Negro American." *Phylon* 15:21–28.

———. "The Tragic Mulatto Theme in Six Works by Langston Hughes." *Phylon* 16:195–204.

———. "Integration and Race Literature." *Phylon* 17:141–46.

———. "Langston Hughes: Cool Poet." *CLA Journal* 40:280–96.

Diakhaté, Lamine. "Langston Hughes, conquerant de l'espoir." *Présence Africaine* 64:38–46.

Dickinson, Donald C. *A Bio-Bibliography of Langston Hughes, 1902-1967.* Hamden, Conn.: Shoe String, 1967.

Dodat, François. *Langston Hughes.* Paris: Édition Seghers, 1964.

Du Bois, W. E. B. and Locke, Alain. "The Younger Literary Movement." *Crisis* 27:161–63.

Ellison, Martha. "Velvet Voices Feed on Bitter Fruit: A Study of American Negro Poetry." *Poet and Critic* 4:39–49.

Emanuel, James. "Langston Hughes' First Short Story: 'Mary Winosky.' " *Phylon* 22:267–72.

———. *Langston Hughes.* New York: Twayne, 1967.

———. "Soul in the Works of Langston Hughes." *Negro Digest* 16:25–30, 74–92.

———. " 'Bodies in the Moonlight': A Critical Analysis." *Readers and Writers* 1:38–39, 42.

———. "The Short Fiction of Langston Hughes." *Freedomways* 8:170–78.

———. "The Literary Experiments of Langston Hughes." *CLA Journal* 11:335–44.

Embree, Edwin. *Thirteen Against the Odds.* New York: Viking, 1944.

Felgar, Robert. "Black Content, White Form." *Studies in Black Literature* 5:28–31.

Filatova, Lydia. "Langston Hughes: American Writer." *International Literature* 1:103–5.

Finger, Hans. "Zwei Beispiele moderner amerikanischer Negerlyrik: Langston Hughes, 'Mother to Son' and Russell Atkins, 'Poem.' " *Literatur in Wissenschaft und Unterricht* 2:38–46.

Fontaine, William T. "The Negro Continuum from Dominant Wish to Collective Act." *Africa Forum* 4:63–96.

Ford, Nick Aaron. "The Negro Novel as a Vehicle of Propaganda." *Quarterly Review of Higher Education among Negroes* 9:135–39.

———. "Battle of the Books: A Critical Survey of Significant Books by and about Negroes published in 1960." *Phylon* 22:119–34.

———. "Search for Identity: A Critical Survey of Significant Belles-

Lettres by and about Negroes published in 1960." *Phylon* 22:128–38.

Furay, Michael. "Africa in Negro American Poetry to 1929." *African Literature Today* No. 1(June 1968), No. 2(Jan. 1969).

Garber, Earlene D. "Form as a Complement to Content in Three of Langston Hughes' Poems." *Negro American Literature Forum* 5:137–39.

Gates, Skip. "Of Negroes Old and New." *Transition* 46:44–57.

Gayle, Addison. "Langston Hughes: A Simple Commentary." *Negro Digest* 16:53–57.

Gibson, Donald B. "The Good Black Poet and the Good Gray Poet: The Poetry of Hughes and Whitman." In *Langston Hughes: Black Genius*, edited by Therman B. O'Daniel. New York: Morrow, 1971.

———, ed. *Five Black Writers: Essays on Wright, Ellison, Baldwin, Hughes, and LeRoi Jones*. New York: New York Univ. Pr., 1970.

———, ed. *Modern Black Poets: A Collection of Essays*. New York: Prentice-Hall, 1973.

Glicksberg, Charles. "Negro Fiction in America." *South Atlantic Quarterly* 45:477–88.

Gloster, Hugh. *Negro Voices in American Fiction*. Chapel Hill: Univ. of North Carolina Pr., 1966.

Govan, Sandra. "The Poetry of the Black Experience as Counterpoint to the Poetry of the Black Aesthetic." *Negro American Literature Forum* 8:288–92.

Gross, Seymour L., and Hardy, John Edward, eds. *Images of the Negro in American Literature*. Chicago: Univ. of Chicago Pr., 1966.

Guillén, Nicolás. "Le Souvenir de Langston Hughes." *Présence Africaine* 44:34–37.

Hampton, Bill. "On Identification with Negro Tricksters." *Southern Folklore Quarterly* 31:55–65.

Hill, Herbert, ed. *Soon One Morning*. New York: Knopf, 1963.

———, ed. *Anger, and Beyond*. New York: Harper, 1966.

Holmes, Eugene. "The Legacy of Alain Locke." *Freedomways* 3:293–306.

———. "Langston Hughes: Philosopher-Poet." *Freedomways* 8:144–51.

Hudson, Theodore. "Langston Hughes' Last Volume of Verse." *CLA Journal* 11:345–48.

———. "Hughes at Columbia." *New Yorker* 43:21–23.

Huggins, Nathan. *Harlem Renaissance*. New York: Oxford Univ. Pr., 1971.

Jackson, Blyden. "An Essay in Criticism." *Phylon* 11:338–43.

———. "The Continuing Strain: Resume of Negro Literature in 1955." *Phylon* (1956), 35–40.

———. "A Word about Simple." *CLA Journal* 11:310–18.

————. "The Negro's Image of the Universe as Reflected in his Fiction." *CLA Journal* 4:22–31.

————. "A Golden Mean for the Negro Novel." *CLA Journal* 3:81–87.

Jackson, Blyden, and Rubin, Louis D. *Black Poetry in America*. Baton Rouge: Louisiana State Univ. Pr., 1974.

Jahn, Janheinz. *Neo-African Literature: A History of Black Writing*. New York: Grove, 1969.

Jemie, Onwuchekwa. "Dream Deferred: A Comment on Langston Hughes' Poetry." Ph.D. dissertation, Columbia Univ., 1972.

Johnson, Charles S. "Jazz Poetry and Blues." *Carolina Magazine* 58: 16–20.

————. "The Negro Renaissance and its Significance." In *The New Negro Thirty Years Afterward*, edited by Rayford Logan, Eugene Holmes, and C. Franklin Edwards. Washington: Howard Univ. Pr., 1955.

Jones, Eldred. " 'Laughing to Keep from Crying': A Tribute to Langston Hughes." *Présence Africaine* 64:51–55.

Jones, Harry L. "A Danish Tribute to Langston Hughes." *CLA Journal* 11:331–34.

————. "Black Humor and the American Way of Life." *Satire Newsletter* 7:1–4.

Kaiser, Ernest. "The Literature of Harlem." *Freedomways* 3:276–91.

————. "Selected Bibliography of the Published Writings of Langston Hughes." *Freedomways* 8:185–91.

Kamp, Stella. "Langston Hughes Speaks to Young Writers." *Opportunity* 24:73.

Kearns, Francis. "The Un-Angry Langston Hughes." *Yale Review* 60:154–60.

Kent, George. "Langston Hughes and the Afro-American Folk and Cultural Tradition." In *Langston Hughes: Black Genius*, edited by Therman B. O'Daniel. New York: Morrow, 1971.

Kestleloot, Lilyan. "Négritude and its American Sources." *Boston University Journal* 22:54–67.

Killens, John. "Broadway in Black and White." *African Forum* 1: 66–76.

King, Woodie. "Remembering Langston Hughes." *Negro Digest* 18: 27–32, 95–96.

Kinnamon, Keneth. "The Man Who Created Simple." *Nation* 205: 599–601.

Kramer, Aaron. "Robert Burns and Langston Hughes." *Freedomways* 8:159–66.

————. "Langston Hughes and the Example of 'Simple.' " *Black World* 19:35–38.

Larkin, Margaret. "A Poet for the People." *Opportunity* 5:84–85.

Lash, John S. "The American Negro and American Literature: A

Checklist of Significant Commentaries." *Bulletin of Bibliography* 19:12–15, 33–36.

———. "The American Negro in American Literature: A Selected Bibliography of Critical Materials." *Journal of Negro Education* 15:722–30.

———. "The Race Consciousness of the American Negro Author: Toward a Reexamination of an Orthodox Critical Concept." *Social Forces* 28:24–34.

———. "A Long, Hard Look at the Ghetto: A Critical Summary of Literature by and About Negroes in 1956." *Phylon* 18:7–24.

———. "Dimension in Racial Experience: A Critical Summary of Literature by and about Negroes in 1958." *Phylon* 20:115–31.

Lieberman, Laurence. "Poetry Chronicle." *Poetry* 112:337–43.

Littlejohn, David. *Black on White: A Critical Survey of Writing by American Negroes.* New York: Grossman, 1966.

Locke, Alain, ed. *The New Negro: An Interpretation.* New York: Albert and Charles Boni, 1925.

Locke, Alain. *Four Negro Poets.* New York: Simon and Schuster, 1927.

———. "The Negro Poets of the United States." In *Anthology of Magazine Verse for 1926 and Yearbook of Poetry,* edited by William Stanley Braithwaite. Boston: B. J. Brimmer, 1927.

———. "The Negro's Contribution to American Art and Literature." *Annals of the American Academy of Political and Social Science* 140:234–47.

———. "The Negro in American Culture." In *Anthology of American Negro Literature,* edited by V. F. Calverton. New York: Modern Library, 1929.

———. "This Year of Grace: Outstanding Books of the Year in Negro Literature." *Opportunity* 9:48–51.

———. "We Turn to Prose: A Retrospective Review of the Literature of the Negro for 1931." *Opportunity* 10:40–44.

———. "Black Truth and Black Beauty: A Retrospective Review of the Literature of the Negro for 1932." *Opportunity* 11:14–18.

———. "The Eleventh Hour of Nordicism." *Opportunity* 13:4–10; part 2, 46–48, 59.

———. "Deep River, Deeper Sea: Retrospective Review of the Literature of the Negro for 1935." *Opportunity* 14:6–10; part 2, 42–43, 61.

———. "The Negro: 'New' or Newer: A Retrospective Review of the Literature of the Negro for 1938." *Opportunity* 17:4–11; part 2, 36–42.

———. "Dry Fields and Green Pastures." *Opportunity* 18:4–10; part 2, 41–46, 53.

———. "Of Native Sons: Real and Otherwise." *Opportunity* 19: 4–9; part 2, 48–52.

————. "A Contribution to American Culture." *Opportunity* 23: 192–93, 238.

————. "The Negro Minority in American Literature." *English Journal* 35:315–19.

————. "Wisdom *de Profundis:* The Literature of the Negro, 1949." *Phylon* 11:5–14.

————. "High Price of Integration." *Phylon* 8:7–16.

————. "From *Native Son* to *Invisible Man:* A Review of the Literature of the Negro for 1952." *Phylon* 14:34–44.

MacLeod, Norman. "The Poetry and Argument of Langston Hughes." *Crisis* 45:358–59.

Margolies, Edward. *Native Sons: A Critical Study of Twentieth Century Negro American Authors.* New York: Lippincott, 1968.

Matheus, John F. "Langston Hughes as Translator." *CLA Journal* 11: 319–30.

McGhee, Nancy. "Langston Hughes: Poet in the Folk Manner." In *Langston Hughes: Black Genius,* edited by Therman B. O'Daniel. New York: Morrow, 1971.

Meltzer, Milton. *Langston Hughes: A Bibliography.* New York: Crowell, 1968.

Miller, Johnine Brown. "The Major Themes in Langston Hughes's *Not Without Laughter.*" *CEA Critic* 32:8–10.

Mintz, Lawrence E. "Langston Hughes's Jesse B. Semple: The Urban Negro as Wise Fool." *Satire Newsletter* 7:11–21.

Mitchell, Loften. *Black Drama: The Story of the American Negro in the Theatre.* New York: Hawthorn, 1967.

————. "For Langston Hughes and Stella Holt: An Informal Memoir." *Negro Digest* 12:41–43, 74–77.

Moore, Gerald. "Poetry in the Harlem Renaissance." In *The Black American Writer,* edited by C. W. E. Bigsby. Deland, Fla.: n.p., 1969.

Moore, Richard B. "Africa Conscious Harlem." *Freedomways* 3: 315–34.

Morris, Lloyd. "The Negro 'Renaissance'," *Southern Workman* 59: 82–86.

Myers, Elisabeth. *Langston Hughes: Poet of His People.* Champaign, Ill.: Garrard, 1970.

Ngandu, Pius. "Le role des noirs américains dans la literature négro-africaine." *Congo-Afrique* 2:337–44.

Nichols, Lewis. "Langston Hughes Describes the Genesis of his 'Tambourines to Glory.' " *New York Times* (Oct. 27, 1963), sect. 2, p. 3.

Noble, Enrique. *Nicolas Guillén y Langston Hughes.* Havana, Cuba: n.p., 1962.

O'Daniel, Therman. "A Langston Hughes Bibliography." *CLA Bulletin* 7:12–13.

————. "Langston Hughes: A Selected Classified Bibliography." *CLA Journal* 11:349–66.

————, ed. *Langston Hughes: Black Genius*. New York: Morrow, 1971.

Osofsky, Gilbert. "Symbols of the Jazz Age: The New Negro and Harlem Discovered." *American Quarterly* 17:229–36.

Parker, John W. "Tomorrow in the Writing of Langston Hughes." *College English* 10:438–41.

Patterson, Lindsay. "Langston Hughes—An Aspirer of Young Writers." *Freedomways* 8:179–81.

Patterson, Louise. "With Langston Hughes in the USSR." *Freedomways* 8:152–58.

Piquion, Rene. *Langston Hughes: Un Chant Nouveau*. Introduction by Arna Bontemps. Port-au-Prince, Haiti: Imprimerie de l'Etat, 1940.

Pool, Rosey. "The Discovery of American Negro Poetry." *Freedomways* 3:511–17.

Presley, James. "The American Dream of Langston Hughes." *Southwest Review* 48:380–86.

Quinot, Raymond. *Langston Hughes*. Brussels: n.p., 1964.

Randall, Dudley. "Three Giants Gone." *Negro Digest* 16:87.

Redding, Saunders. *To Make a Poet Black*. Chapel Hill: Univ. of North Carolina Pr., 1939.

Redmond, Eugene B. "The Black American Epic: Its Roots, Its Writers." *Black Scholar* 2:15–22.

Rive, Richard. "Taos in Harlem: An Interview with Langston Hughes." *Contrast* 14:33–39.

Rollins, Charlemae. *Black Troubadour: Langston Hughes*. Chicago: Rand McNally, 1970.

Rosenblatt, Roger. *Black Fiction*. Cambridge: Harvard Univ. Pr., 1974.

Salkey, Andrew. "To Langston Hughes." *Présence Africaine* 44:56.

Schatt, Stanley. "Langston Hughes: The Minstrel as Artificer." *Journal of Modern Literature* 4:115–20.

Shelton, Robert. "Theatre." *Nation* 196:20.

Smalley, Webster, ed. *Five Plays by Langston Hughes*. Bloomington: Indiana Univ. Pr., 1963.

Smith, Raymond. "Langston Hughes: Evolution of the Poetic Personae." *Studies in the Literary Imagination* 7:49–64.

Spencer, T. J., and Rivers, Clarence. "Langston Hughes: His Style and His Optimism." *Drama Critique* 7:99–102.

Staples, Elizabeth. "Langston Hughes: Malevolent Force." *American Mercury* 98:46–50.

Thurman, Wallace. "Negro Artists and the Negro." *New Republic* 52:37–39.

————. "Nephews of Uncle Remus." *Independent* 99:296–98.

————. "Negro Poets and Their Poetry." *Bookman* 67:555–61.

Turner, Darwin. "Langston Hughes as Playwright." *CLA Journal* 11:297–309.

————. "*The Negro Novel in America:* In Rebuttal." *CLA Journal* 10:122–34.

————. "The Negro Dramatist's Image of the Universe, 1920-1960." *CLA Journal* 5:106–20.

Turpin, Waters E. "Four Short Fiction Writers of the Harlem Renaissance—Their Legacy of Achievement." *CLA Journal* 11:59–72.

Wagner, Jean. "Langston Hughes." *Information and Documents* (Paris) 135:30–35.

————. *Les Poètes Négres des États-Unis*. Paris: Librairie Ista., 1962.

————. *Black Poets of the United States*. Translated by Kenneth Douglas. Urbana: Univ. of Illinois Pr., 1973.

Waldron, Edward. "The Blues Poetry of Langston Hughes." *Negro American Literature Forum* 5:140–49.

Walker, Margaret. "New Poets." *Phylon* 11:345–54.

Welburn, Ron. "Nationalism and Internationalism in Black Literature: The Afro-American Scene." *Greenfield Review* 3:60–72.

Whitlow, Roger. *Black American Literature: A Critical History*. Totowa, N.J.: Littlefield, 1974.

Williams, Kenny. *They Also Spoke: An Essay on Negro Literature in America, 1787-1930*. Nashville, Tenn.: Townsend, 1970.

Winslow, Vernon. "Negro Art and the Depression." *Opportunity* 19:40–42, 62–63.

Yestadt, Marie. "Two American Poets: Their Influence on the Contemporary Art Song." *Xavier University Studies* 10:33–43.

Yoseloff, Thomas, ed. *Seven Poets in Search of an Answer*. New York: B. Ackerman, 1944.

Young, James O. *Black Writers of the Thirties*. Baton Rouge: Louisiana State Univ. Pr., 1973.

Index